THIRD EDITION—Revised & Updated

Over 250,000 sold in 20 languages

Ten Things
Every Child
with Autism
Wishes You Knew

ELLEN NOTBOHM

Ten Things Every Child with Autism Wishes You Knew, Third Edition
All marketing and publishing rights guaranteed to and reserved by:

FUTURE HORIZONS INC.

(800) 489-0727
(817) 277-0727
(817) 277-2270 (fax)
E-mail: info@fhautism.com
www.fhautism.com

© 2019 Ellen Notbohm
Website: https://ellennotbohm.com
Email: emailme@ellennotbohm.com
Social media: Facebook, Instagram, Twitter, LinkedIn, Pinterest

For foreign rights licensing, please contact the author at emailme@ellennotbohm.com

ISBN: 9781941765883

Praise for
Ten Things Every Child with Autism Wishes You Knew

"This third edition is amazing, and an absolute must-read. Ellen has absorbed so much more wisdom from both the autism world and the autistic world and poured it into her work, and I'm floored. Buy this book, read it, loan it, share it, then read it again!"

— Jennifer McIlwee Myers, Author of *Growing Up with Sensory Issues: Insider Tips from a Woman with Autism* and *How to Teach Life Skills to Kids with Autism or Asperger's*

"This third edition of *Ten Things Every Child with Autism Wishes You Knew* is without exception the best yet! As an international consultant on ASD who works with individuals, schools, and parents, I have used this resource as a core teaching tool in most of my trainings, especially with staff who are new to the field of Special Education and/or working with an individual with ASD. I was really excited to see the new chapter on Your Power of Choice. As Ellen writes: 'Seldom is the instance in which we truly have no choices,' and this is so true. It empowers the individual to have control in a world that in many ways feels out of control. This book is a must have for your autism resource collection."

— Jim Ball, EdD, BCBA-D, President/CEO JB Autism Consulting

"I wouldn't have believed that Ellen Notbohm could improve on her original classic, the excellent *Ten Things Every Child with Autism Wishes You Knew*, but she has done just that. As a parent, as one who works with autistic people, and as an avid reader on the subject, I'm telling you: you must have this book on your shelf. If you know anyone on the spectrum, this book will help you understand them better. Parents who made it through your child's early years with hope and optimism intact because you had the original *Ten Things*, you need this update. Notbohm will take you from the preschool years through middle school, high school, and beyond, continuing to inform and inspire parents as they prepare their children for adulthood. The questions for discussion and reflection are perfect for parent support groups, teacher trainings, or book clubs. Optimism abounds."

— Wendela Whitcomb Marsh, MA, BCBA, RSD, Author of *The ABC's of Autism in the Classroom*

"The new edition of *Ten Things Every Child with Autism Wishes You Knew* is better than ever. This is essential reading for people who are important in your child's life, be it teachers, therapists, family members, neighbors and even the bus driver, to help them understand your child's complex and sometimes baffling social, sensory, behavioral, and emotional challenges. Written by the mother of two sons on the spectrum, this book gives a powerful voice to kids, teens, and adults who can't easily advocate for themselves, providing an 'inside view' of the different realities of life with autism. The new chapter on 'Your Power of Choice' compassionately helps readers recognize that while they may feel overwhelmed, scared, and sometimes paralyzed, they are never powerless, and provides key empowering steps they can take to help those they love thrive and live meaningful, productive lives."

— Lindsey Biel, Occupational Therapist, Coauthor of *Raising a Sensory Smart Child: The Definitive Book for Helping Your Child with Sensory Processing Issues,* Author of *Sensory Processing Strategies: Effective Clinical Work with Kids & Teens*

"Every child with autism deserves to have the adults in their life read this book. Parents will find a compassionate, astute ally who has lived the journey with her now-adult son. All readers will clarify and refine their understanding of what it really takes to help a child fit into the world, achieve a state of confidence, and fulfill their unique promise. Compact, well organized and accessible, *Ten Things Every Child with Autism Wishes You Knew* contains a remarkable amount of detailed information, helpful suggestions, and concrete strategies. Realistic, practical, and uplifting, it will help you make the best choices for both your child and yourself. It is on my 'short list' of highly recommended books on autism and

I urge you to soak up its wisdom and then share it with others."

— Debra Moore, PhD, Psychologist (retired) and Coauthor with Temple Grandin
of *The Loving Push: How Parents and Professionals Can Help Spectrum Kids
Become Successful Adults*

"Ellen Notbohm reminds us once again that we should learn more than we teach and that we should listen more than we talk. *Ten Things* emphasizes these points and offers readers important insights and invaluable information. If you have a 1st or 2nd edition, you will want to purchase a new copy as this book is not just a compassionate and person-centered look at autism, it is also a reflection of a changing field and evolving understandings of advocacy, support, and ability."

— Paula Kluth, PhD, Author of *You're Going to Love This Kid* and *Pedro's Whale*

"Great book for the parent of a child who is newly diagnosed. It will help the parent who is frightened by the diagnosis get started on creating a positive outcome for their child."

— Temple Grandin, PhD, Author of *The Way I See It* and *Thinking in Pictures*

"The third edition explains our evolving insights into autism that are so valuable for parents, professionals, and those who have autism. Please grant the wish of the autistic child that you know and absorb the wisdom and clarity of a book that I highly recommend."

— Tony Attwood, PhD, Author of *Ask Dr. Tony: Answers from the World's
Leading Authority on Asperger's Syndrome/High-Functioning Autism*

"How wonderful that Ellen Notbohm's classic, *Ten Things Every Child with Autism Wishes You Knew*, is here for a new generation! If your child has been diagnosed with autism, or if you think that your child may have autism, this is the first book that you should read."

— Bobbi Sheahan, Author of *What I Wish I'd Known about Raising a Child
with Autism*

Praise for *Ten Things Every Child with Autism Wishes You Knew*

"When my son was diagnosed, I was overwhelmed, heartbroken, and confused. A day or so later, I picked up *Ten Things* and it was a breath of fresh air. I didn't need piles of medical texts and studies at that point in time, I needed what this book gave me—understanding, compassion, and hope."

— Karen Topper

"*Ten Things* is the book I found most helpful and most hopeful after my son's autism diagnosis eight years ago. Since then, I have recommended it to many parents at the start of their journey and, like me, they have fallen completely in love with it."

— Maura Campbell, Senior Editor, *Spectrum Women* magazine

Also by Ellen Notbohm

Nonfiction

1001 Great Ideas for Teaching and Raising Children with
Autism or Asperger's
with co-author Veronica Zysk

Ten Things Your Student with Autism Wishes You Knew
with Veronica Zysk

The Autism Trail Guide: Postcards from the Road Less Traveled

Fiction

The River by Starlight

For Connor and Bryce

because they are doing such a commendable job of raising me

Contents

Preface

When *Children's Voice* published my article "Ten Things Every Child with Autism Wishes You Knew" in 2004, I couldn't have anticipated the response. Reader after reader wrote to tell me that the piece should be required reading for all social-service workers, teachers, therapists, and relatives of children with autism. "Just what my daughter would say if she could," said one mother. "Screams wisdom throughout every word and sentence," said another. The article traveled from website to website, around the world, crisscrossing every continent (except Antarctica). The sheer volume of interest and the diversity of the groups who found it relevant humbled me. They included hundreds of autism and Asperger's groups, but also support groups for chronic pain, obesity, assistance dogs, inner ear disorders, homeschoolers, religious school educators, knitting circles, food retailers. "I have a strong sense that your message crosses over to many special needs," wrote a social worker in the American Midwest.

"Ten Things" quickly took on a life of its own. Why was it resonating so loudly? I decided that it came from the fact that the piece spoke with a child's voice, a voice largely unheard in the rising uproar about autism. The often-tumultuous dialogue was, and still is, productive and welcome. But what could be more ironic than that the subjects of the discussion are often exemplified by the inability to express and advocate for themselves? I had seen several articles that took related approaches: ten things teachers want parents to know, or what mothers wish their children's teachers knew, what dads of autistic children need to know. When my editor, Veronica Zysk, presented me with one such adult-to-adult piece, I asked, who speaks for the child?

"Write that piece," Veronica urged.

My son Bryce had been formally diagnosed at age four. I felt fortunate that his voice had been heard, thanks to committed teamwork among family members, school staff, and community resource workers. I ardently wanted his level of success to be the norm, not the exception. The original article, and later, the original edition of this book, flowed from that.

Individual and collective attitudes about autism form under the influence of the language we choose in defining it. The incendiary and provocative remarks and opinions, whether intentional or thoughtless, commandeer our attention. We may respond to them, we may despair of them, we may choose to ignore them. But it may be the squadron of subtleties and nuances of language flying under our radar that does more to impede the development of healthy outlooks about a child's autism. Throughout the book, you'll be asked to contemplate how the language of autism shapes your perspective. It will help you view autism from angles you may not have yet considered. There are also a few things you won't see.

You won't see the word "autism" capitalized in this book unless it's at the beginning of a sentence or part of a name or title. We don't capitalize breast cancer, diabetes, glaucoma, anorexia, depression, or other conditions that don't include someone's name, like Asperger's. Capitalizing "autism" makes a visual statement that assigns it an authority and power it doesn't deserve.

You won't see these words used to describe a child with autism: suffer, obsess, perfect, picky, tantrum, quirky, or other words that perpetuate derogatory stereotypes, or stereotypes that set unrealistic, unfounded or unattainably high expectations.

And finally, the word "normal" never appears in this book outside quotation marks. The early days following our son's diagnosis of autism were spiked with questions from others along the lines of

"Do you think he'll ever learn to be normal?" I found these questions at first stupefying, and later, presumptuous in a manner that almost made me pity the asker. I learned to answer the question with a smile and a wink and "When there comes a time that there is such a thing" or "Naw, he'll never be a dryer setting." Then and now, I quoted Canadian songwriter Bruce Cockburn, who put it, "the trouble with normal is it always gets worse."

"A Word about Normal" is my favorite passage from the book Veronica and I later wrote together, *1001 Great Ideas for Teaching and Raising Children with Autism and Asperger's*. In it, a middle school speech therapist answers a mother's concern that her son hasn't made many friends and might not "do all the normal teen things we did."

> "When your son came to me last year," the speech therapist tells Mom, "his social thinking skills were almost nonexistent. He didn't understand why he should say hi to people in the halls, he didn't know how to ask a question to further a conversation, or how to engage with a peer during the lunch hour. Now he's working on those things. That's a huge amount of progress."
>
> "But he's only made two friends."
>
> "I would rephrase that: he's made two friends! One shares his interest in model trains and one shares his interest in running. He knows how you feel, though. So I am going to share with you what he told me the other day. He said, 'I don't want a lot of friends. I can't handle a lot of friends. More than one at a time stresses me out. I can talk to these

two friends about things I'm interested in. They are great for me.'

"Walk through this or any other school," the SLP continues. "You'll see a huge range of 'normal' middle school behavior. You'll see nerdy normal, sporty normal, musical normal, artsy normal, techie normal. Kids tend to gravitate to groups that make them feel safe. For now, your son has found his group. You and I walk a fine line: honoring his choices while continuing to teach him the skills he needs to feel comfortable expanding his boundaries."

Your child has many social selves. To embrace all of them, and therefore him as a whole child, is to redefine how we view "normal"—one person at a time.

Although the ten things presented in this book characterized my child, they won't and can't possibly apply in total to all children with autism. Rather, you'll see some of the characteristics and needs in every child on the autism spectrum in degrees that vary from child to child, and from hour to hour, day to day, and year to year in an individual child. Sometimes they overlap, or manifest differently when context or setting changes, socially or physically. So you may notice that I'll sometimes make a particular point more than one way in this book. It's not careless repetition or redundancy, it's deliberate recognition that often we need to hear something more than once or approach it in more than one way to fully understand and process it. We have to acknowledge this in ourselves to be able to do the same for our children, because this is an essential component of being able to teach autistic children in a manner meaningful to them. It's the threshold to a world of choice, for you and your child, much more expansive that you might at first imagine.

With education, therapy, growth and development—yours included—the limitations imposed by some of these character-istics may diminish, and some of those so-called limitations may be re-channeled in such a manner that you come to see them as strengths. When you reach the end of this book and in the days that follow, you may find yourself in a new and more interesting place on your child's autism spectrum than where you started. I hope so.

So, why a third edition of *Ten Things Every Child with Autism Wishes You Knew* when millions have read the first and second editions and the book's appeal remains strong? Why fix something that isn't broken? In his book and film *Journey of the Universe*, evolutionary philosopher Brian Thomas Swimme describes the Milky Way galaxy "not as a thing, but as an ongoing activity." Such is the autism spectrum, an ever-exchanging sphere of being within a larger universe. We travel the continuum, sometimes hurtling along, sometimes stalling out, but each particle—child, parent, teacher, sibling, grandparent, friend, stranger—has his or her own place in the (sometimes elusive) order of things. That spot on the spectrum shifts over time.

Experience and maturity change our perspective. The years that passed between the first and second editions of *Ten Things* encom-passed my son's post-high school years and transition to adulthood, including learning to drive, becoming a voter, stepping into the often-irrational world of dating, attending college and joining the workplace. How could that not have altered my position on the spectrum? Those years also saw a continuing global increase in autism spectrum disorders that baffled and alarmed everyone with a pulse (everyone but the cult-level cynics). My place on the spectrum shifted in the face of my own experiences, but also in response to the experiences of others who came into my life because of *Ten Things*.

Autism is as complex as it ever was, and the sheer number of autistic children among us—who, barring catastrophe, will become autistic adults wanting to take their rightful, meaningful place in community—demands attention even from those who would rather turn their conscience and public dollars away. We defend and advocate for our children with more eyes upon us than we did just a decade ago. By conscription, we have become not just advocates, but emissaries. Being a parent of an autistic child today requires not only stamina, curiosity, creativity, patience, resilience, and diplomacy, but the courage to think expansively and to dream accordingly.

Being a parent of an autistic child today requires the courage to think expansively and dream accordingly.

The years since the second edition of *Ten Things* have also seen an explosion in social media communication that's impossible to ignore. The amount of information and opinion coming at parents of autistic children is a never-ending tsunami of ever-changing, maybe-this maybe-that. There have always been charlatans, hucksters and hysterics among us, but nowadays it is much harder to sift the useful information from the click-bait, the truths from the half-truths and the pants-on-fires. Yet we still have only the same twenty-four hours in a day we ever had. More urgently than ever, parents want and need succinct and easily digestible information, especially at the start of their autism journey. My response has been to update and streamline *Ten Things*, refocus on the basic and the essential, with a new and robust emphasis on honing one of the most important powers you have: the power of choice, and how to use it to make the best decisions for your child from amidst the array of alternatives and possibilities that extends from "no choice" to "overwhelming number of choices."

Thus, a third edition of *Ten Things*, faithful to its core being but speaking to our changing times. That core is the timeless, borderless, cross-cultural nature of the ten things.

Throughout the book, I've described how my perspective has changed since early editions of the book. These are not "back in the day" musings for the sake of nostalgia, or shades-of-subtle jibes intended to make you aware of how much easier you have it today compared to parents of earlier decades. Far more important than my mere personal opinion, these perspective shifts vividly illustrate how much things change over time, how influenced we can be— for better or worse—when technology, education and medicine advance, stall out, or fail, and how your own developmental journey through the spectrum and the universe shapes your inner being and world view. I think my attitude shifts aren't particularly remarkable given all I've experienced and all we've learned about autism over the last fifteen years. But once in a while someone will remark that I've "flip-flopped."

Don't let anyone persuade you that adopting a different attitude based on new experiences and information is "flip-flopping." Quite the opposite, the inability or unwillingness to think flexibly—and to expect it of others—is the kind of rigidity that hurts our kids, and society. (Ironically, that rigidity and lack of flexible thinking is what many people disdain and despair of in autistic children.) We can remain true to our core values while embracing expanded perspective and growth of soul, and encouraging the same in our children. It's called adapting. It's called learning, becoming hopefully wiser, becoming more whole in how we view autism and the challenges it presents to our children. Remember that the idea we often attribute to Darwin, "survival of the fittest," doesn't mean the strongest or the smartest or luckiest, but the ones best able to acclimate to change.

Who speaks for the child? It requires a level of presumption to think that any of us can get inside someone else's head and speak for them. I take that risk, in light of the overwhelming need to understand the world as the child with autism experiences it. It falls on us to grant legitimacy and worth to their different way of thinking, communicating, and navigating the world. It demands that we give voice to their thoughts and feelings, knowing that those voices may be nonspeaking or otherwise nonverbal. If we don't, the legacy of our children's autism will be opportunities untouched, gifts forever undiscovered. They are our call to action.

It begins...

As the mother of a young child with autism, I quickly learned that on some days, the only predictable thing was the unpredictability; the only consistent attribute—the inconsistency. Much of autism still baffles us, despite the advances that have been made in our understanding of its spectrum nature. Yet, day to day and sometimes moment to moment, we still find ourselves bewildered by behaviors both new and recurrent that our autistic children exhibit, no matter how hard we try to see the world through their eyes.

Not so very long ago, professionals thought autism to be an "incurable disorder." The notion of autism as an intractable condition with which no person can live meaningfully and productively has crumbled in the face of knowledge and understanding that continue to increase even as you read this. Every day, autistic individuals show us that they can overcome, compensate for, and otherwise manage many of their autism's most challenging aspects as part of their fulfilling and dynamic lives. Many of them not only don't seek a "cure," but reject the concept. In a widely read *New York Times* article in December 2004, Jack Thomas, a tenth grader with Asperger's syndrome, got the world's attention by stating, "We don't have a disease, so we can't be cured. This is just the way we are." Today, social and mainstream media reverberates with the cogent voices of autistic adults who affirm and embrace Jack's position.

I stand with them. When nonautistic people frame the challenges of autism only through the lens of their own experiences, they unwittingly close the door to the kind of alternative thinking that will profoundly affect, perhaps even make or break, their children's futures.

Perspective is everything. When I speak to parent groups, I ask them to jot down brief descriptions of their children's most challenging behaviors, and then rephrase them in the positive. Is the child stand-offish—or able to entertain herself and work independently? Is she reckless—or adventuresome and willing to try new experiences? Is she compulsively neat—or does she have outstanding organizational skills? Does she pester you with endless questions—or does she have a curiosity about her world as well as tenacity and persistence? Why do we try to fix the kid who perseverates but admire the one who perseveres? Both are forms of the same word meaning "refuses to stop."

My family's journey across the spectrum began with a basically sweet-tempered but nonverbal child who would lapse into bewildering meltdowns. He backed away from many activities with his hands over his ears. He wore clothes only when socially necessary and didn't seem to experience pain or cold in a typical way.

A public school early intervention team identified Bryce's autism at age three. I went through the five stages of grief in the time it took to end the initial meeting. My older son Connor had been identified two years earlier with attention deficit/hyperactivity disorder (ADHD). I already knew about the therapies, the social challenges, the never-ending vigilance—and the exhaustion.

Raw fear motivated me. I couldn't bear to imagine Bryce's fate as an adult if I didn't do everything within my power to equip him to live in a world where I wouldn't always be around. I couldn't rid my head of words like "prison" and "homeless." Not for a nanosecond did it occur to me to leave his future to the professionals or to the ephemeral idea that he might outgrow his autism. These thoughts propelled me out of bed every morning and drove me to take the actions I did.

Jump a few years ahead with me now to the turn of the twenty-first century. At the school assembly, adorable first graders step to the microphone one after another to answer the question, "What do you want to be in the new millennium?" A soccer star! is a popular response. A pop singer! A race car driver! Cartoon artist, veterinarian, firefighter!

Bryce has considered the question carefully.

"I think I'd just like to be a grown-up."

Applause breaks out and the principal speaks deliberately. "The world would be a better place," he says, "if more people aspired to what Bryce aspires to."

Here's the gist of what I know to be true: your child's autism doesn't mean that he, you, and your family won't lead full, joyous, meaningful lives. You may be scared, but dare to believe this, with a caveat. How much of that full measure we achieve with our kids depends on the choices we make for and about them. A memorable passage from Nora Ephron's story *Heartburn* has the protagonist, Rachel Samstat, asserting that when your "dream breaks into a million tiny little pieces, it leaves you with a choice. You can either stick with it, which is unbearable, or you can go off and dream another dream."

We choose.

If you're reading this as a newcomer to the world of autism, I say, autism itself is not awful. Not understanding it, not having people around you who understand it, not getting the help that's out there for your child—that can be very awful. You're at the beginning of a long journey. This book will alert you to signposts you will likely pass along the way, so that when you do, they'll have a familiar look to them and be less foreign and frightening.

This book can help speak for you and your child to those who need to hear your message: teachers, parents, siblings, in-laws, babysitters, coaches, bus drivers, peer parents, friends of siblings, clergy, neighbors. It can help equip those around our children with basic understanding of autism's common elements. That understanding has a tremendous impact on our children's ability to progress toward productive, independent adulthood.

Autism is complex, but in this book, its myriad characteristics fall into four fundamental areas: sensory processing, communication, social comprehension and interaction skills, and whole-child self-esteem issues. All are crucial. Here's why:

Sensory processing. Autistic persons of all ages experience sensory hyper- and/or hypo-sensitivity reactions, sometimes consistent and predictable, sometimes variant and unpredictable. The implication and effect this has is inescapable. A child can't be expected to absorb cognitive or social learning, or "behave," when he experiences his environment as a constant bombardment of unpleasant sensations and nasty surprises. Your brain filters thousands of multiple-sensory inputs (what you see, hear, smell, touch, etc.) simultaneously. His does not. It can provoke the equivalent of twenty-four-hour road rage as all those signals jam in the brain stem. Think of how you feel trapped in the stifling fumes and racket of stalled traffic with no ability to affect your situation.

Communication. Language development delays can be prevalent in children with autism. Without adequate functional means of expression, their needs and wants remain unmet. The inevitable result is anger and frustration, not learning and growing. The ability to communicate, whether through spoken language, pictures, signing, or assistive technology, is bedrock, because it's inarguable that all children have thoughts that require expression. The assumption that a child who can't communicate has nothing to say is as patently ridiculous as assuming an adult without a car has nowhere to go.

Social comprehension and interaction skills. Elusive and ephemeral, these skills can differ from culture to culture, from setting to setting within a culture, and from relationship to relationship, even from hour to hour. The inability to use social attention and interpretation to figure out what to say or do in any situation can isolate a child to a devastating degree. The child with autism, who truly doesn't "get it," paddles against a brutal current if we don't provide sustained concrete instruction that makes sense to her social brain, and ongoing opportunities to practice and use the skills in real time.

> **The assumption that a child who can't communicate has nothing to say is as patently ridiculous as assuming an adult without a car has nowhere to go.**

Whole-child self-esteem issues. Every last person on the planet is a package deal. We want to be accepted and appreciated for who we are as a whole, not a bundle of traits to be cherry-picked by others. Your autistic child does need skilled guidance to achieve a comfortable place in the larger world. Working toward that goal with positive energy and optimism doesn't constitute "fixing" the child. Teaching any child, whether "special" or "normal," the skills for success and self-sufficiency isn't "fixing" or "curing," it's helping them learn and master what they need to know and be able to do, to live as independently as possible. It's loving and guiding them through an ongoing learning process with the same acceptance of whole self we want for ourselves.

Bryce's successes spring from that sense of self-esteem, his hard-won comfort with his physical environment and, even in adulthood, his ever-expanding ability to express himself and advocate for himself. As those pieces fell into place through the course of his childhood and adolescence, social and cognitive learning followed. Each passing year brought deeply gratifying feats: the day he swam to a trophy finish in a citywide swim meet, the day he sang and danced his way through *Charlie and the Chocolate Factory* as Grandpa Joe. The day he rode his two-wheeler for the first time. His elation at making it through his first Scout camp out, and his euphoria after working up the nerve to ask the girl he'd admired since kindergarten to dance at the sock hop. Running, running through six years on middle school and high school track teams. Earning his first paycheck. Travelling solo. Getting his driver's license. Hanging his college diploma on the wall.

Though the four elements we've just discussed may be common to many autistic children, keep in mind that the reason we call it a spectrum is that no two kids will be completely alike. Each will begin the journey at a different point on that spectrum, and each will travel their developmental trajectory at a pace and with a perspective uniquely their own, and 100% legitimate. And, just as importantly, every parent, teacher, and caregiver will be at a unique point in their understanding of the spectrum. Like the millions of pixels that comprise a television image, each person involved is a complicated composite. That's why there is no single recipe for success, no substitute for the research, self-education, and legwork necessary, and little window for complacency. Guiding, educating and appreciating the child with autism will be a continual work-in-progress.

The revered opera diva Beverly Sills, mother of two special needs children, once said, "There is no shortcut to anyplace worth going." True, but the journey can be steeped in the joy of discovery. The guidebook is in your hands.

Chapter One

I am a whole child.

My autism is part of who I am, not all of who I am. Are you just one thing, or are you a person with thoughts, feelings, ideas, likes and dislikes, talents, and dreams? Are you fat (overweight), near-sighted (wear glasses) or clumsy (uncoordinated)? Those may be things I see first when I meet you, but you're more than just that, aren't you?

I'm a child, learning and growing. Neither you nor I yet know what I may be capable of. If you think of me as just one thing, you run the danger of setting up an expectation that may be too low. And if I get a sense that you don't think I "can do it," my response will be, why try?

"**A**re you familiar with the term 'autism?'"

That question from Bryce's early childhood special education teacher marked the first time I heard the word autism applied to my child. For me, as for many parents, it was a scary moment, because that one word scrambled my image of my child's future and tossed it into unsurveyed terrain. Fear of the unknown can be one of the most penetrating dreads in the human experience, but in that first daunting moment, the October sun pierced the wall of windows behind me and settled like a reassuring hand on my back. Against the dark monolith of all I didn't know about autism, one luminous thing I did know shone through: my son was the same child I had fallen in love with the day I learned he was on the way, and I was the same mother he loved and trusted. Autism couldn't dent that.

No fan am I of gratuitous political correctness, but in those early days, I had to make a decision about how I viewed my child and his autism, and how I would project that view both to the world and to him. Was he a "child with autism" or was he "autistic?" Given that the social perceptions of the time were based largely on misconceptions, I saw it as an honest confrontation of how words can be accurate and yet set up expectations or preconceived notions that seriously impede a child's progress toward attainable long-range goals.

When my family stepped onto the spectrum in the mid-1990s, parents and professionals within the autism community understood, as we still do today, that when we used the word autistic, we meant "of or relating to autism or a person with autism." But then as now, those of us who live with and love a child with autism also live with the vexing lack of knowledge and unfair stereotypes assigned by the larger world. The incidence of autism at the time of my son's diagnosis was 1 in 750; descriptions of autism as a "rare" and "mysterious" disorder (or worse, "disease") were common. Whether we liked it or not, "autistic" hadn't yet inspired favorable general reactions, didn't yet stir the bystander to look beyond the label to see a whole person, splendidly full of both gifts and gaffes. The broader reaction, "Uh-oh. Silent, withdrawn hand-flapper," was too prevalent. The first assumption was generally one of limitations. Or maybe we got the opposite but equally suffocating notion: "Uh-oh. Awkward, antisocial computer/math/music prodigy."

One of the biggest shifts in perception about autism has been brought about by a generation of children diagnosed with autism who have grown up to be a vibrant and vocal population, most of whom vehemently identify as "autistic." They've changed the tone of a word that carried heavily negative connotations when they were children, to a word that's no longer a short-cut adjective, but one by which many define themselves. Their voices are authentic and have changed my thinking about my usage of the word "autistic." But it's important to know where we came from, to arrive where we are now.

Where negative or inaccurate descriptions of autism fester, we change perceptions one person at a time. And we begin by asking ourselves: what expectations do words set up?

In the early days of my search for information that would give me some grasp of autism, I came across a ridiculous online dictionary that paired the word "autistic" with the synonym "unfit," and continued with a jaw-dropping list of 155 "related terms," including anesthetized, catatonic, emotionally dead, greedy, heartless, narcissistic, self-besot, soulless, and untouchable. Not one of these words described my child—nor yours, I'll bet.

In the long run—and it is a long run—regardless of what you call it, whether child with autism, autistic child, Aspie, on the spectrum, ASD, what you choose to believe about a child's autism may be the single biggest factor affecting his ultimate outcome. Consciously or otherwise, you make decisions based on your perspective hundreds of times a day. Losing sight of your whole child behind any label makes your life and his more trying. All children spiral through equilibrium and disequilibrium as they cruise the developmental timeline. Most children will test limits, potty-talk in public, elevate stubbornness to Olympic proportions, flush Batman down the toilet, neglect hygiene, and cry when things don't go their way. Attributing it all to autism is not only inaccurate and unfair, it robs you of appreciating the aspects of your child's development that are typical. He has hopes, preferences, likes, dislikes, fears, and dreams like any other child. In time and with teaching, he will be able to tell you about them, albeit maybe not with words.

What you choose to believe about a child's autism may be the single biggest factor affecting his ultimate outcome.

Every child deserves to start his or her life and education with a slate clean of preconceived notions. Even when not malicious, labels are seldom harmless. Consider the varied ways in which putting the adjective before the child colors our expectations and our children's potential.

Too low

"Bryce is getting As in my classes," a teacher told me at our first middle school parent conference. "He does everything asked of him, his homework is never late, he participates enthusiastically in class, and he is never off-task."

He continued: "Bryce has exceeded everything I thought I knew about how much autistic kids can accomplish. I've had autistic kids

4

in my classes. His creativity and organization are far and above the others ..."

His voice tapered off in mid-sentence. "I think I get it," he said. "That word sets up an expectation that's probably lower than what the child is capable of. Am I getting it?"

Yes, he got it, and an already-good teacher got better for every child with autism who came after Bryce. The teacher realized that when he qualified "kid" with "autistic," he set a bar in his mind for what the child couldn't do. Each person who interacts with the child sets the bar at a different place. Whether too low ("You don't think I can do it. Why try?") or too high ("I'm never good enough. Why try?"), should we force the child to travel the extra distance to meet what might be our own ill-conceived expectations? The road is long enough as it is.

Too high

"Autistic today, genius tomorrow."

When this bumper sticker loomed up in front of me on the rump of an SUV, it reminded me that messages perpetuating stereotypes, even when well-intended, are dangerous. In reinforcing a lofty clichéd characterization that most autistic individuals will never achieve, "autistic today, genius tomorrow" sets up for failure the very people it seeks to support. A middle school administrator once told me how much he enjoyed getting to know Bryce, a child with autism who was neither a genius nor a behavior problem. The fact that a seasoned educator found him remarkable is sad, isn't it? Placing the bar too high, setting up a personal or a societal expectation that any day now our autistic child will wake up as a brainiac, more likely creates a parent who motors along without a realistic grasp of the strengths and weaknesses of his/her own child, and a child who will go through life with feelings of chronic inadequacy. Imagine it—the eyes of impatient society following you, collective fingers drumming, waiting for "genius" to show itself. Whether the child is struggling or is happily adjusted to who he is, the expectation of breakthrough greatness is bound to be a(nother) heavy burden.

The mother of a six-year-old told me that of all the questions she fields about her son's autism, the one that rankles most is, "What's his gift?" Some autistic children will someday manifest genius. Most will not. Some people who aren't autistic emerge as geniuses. Most do not. We owe our children faith, conviction, and support, whether or not they'll display "genius tomorrow." Genius doesn't guarantee independence, productivity, or satisfaction in life. We know a young autistic man who has indeed grown up to be a math genius. His mother worries because they are a family of math geniuses— chronically unemployed math geniuses. She's seen how genius doesn't translate into ability to interact effectively with coworkers and clients, to accept direction, set goals, meet deadlines. She'd be happier if her son had a little less genius, a lot more social savvy and some marketable job skills.

Too broad

Here's a peek into my professional life, as it pertains to this discussion. Editors and instructors constantly pummel writers to avoid adjectives, instead to use stronger, more active, more descriptive nouns, verbs and phrases. Such words don't always flow from us writers; it often takes effort to pull up those more specific, more emotive terms. But it always makes for more compelling story-telling. Whether or not you're a writer, you become a storyteller on the day your child is born. How you tell your child's story at each step of his development will determine the type of people drawn to him or her. It will influence who commits to playing a role in it for a page, a chapter or longer, and who tunes out.

Looking back at dozens of IEP meetings and teacher conferences over a span of more than twenty years, I can recall very few times when I, or the seventy-five or so teachers Bryce had, discussed his autism by name. Vivid in my memory are the hundreds of hours and pages of in-depth discussion and strategizing about social-emotional, academic, language, and sensory issues, objectives, and goals. One by one, year by year, we defined, framed, addressed and vanquished each one in terms of measurable success, largely sans labels. In time and with teaching, Bryce learned to be an effective self-advocate—to ask for what he needed, based on his under-standing of his own learning and processing style. The label applied to that learning and processing style wasn't of primary relevance. He viewed his autism as a significant part of himself that would always be so, but also clearly identified aspects of his persona and worldview that might be called "typical" or "regular." He likened himself to *Star Trek*'s Mr. Spock, and how Spock's Vulcan part and human part coexisted in him, coloring the way he experienced both cognitive and social-emotional thinking, sometimes in surprising ways—but always as whole person.

Autism offers few short cuts, few pat answers or glib descriptions for how we represent our child to the world he must inhabit. Through many years of day camps, swim lessons, new teachers, coaches, neighbors, or friends, I didn't open a conversation by describing my son as autistic, but rather offered a short list of how his autism might affect him in the setting, and included communication tactics and accommodations that would give him the best shot at success in each environment. I asked people to speak to him directly, at close range, and without slang or idioms. To show more than tell. To direct his attention to appropriate peer models. These instructions were simple but not simplistic. Those concrete directives gave other people in my son's life tools that made his successes possible.

More recently, a news item caught my eye that illustrated the vastness of the spectrum of abilities within autism. A mom seeking services for her adult son said: "He is almost a savant when it comes to learning facts, but he can't use them." In high school, the young man scored ninety-two percent in pure math, but daily problem-solving gives him difficulty. This mother said it took four years to teach her son to ride the bus alone. In my house, on the other side of the spectrum, Bryce may struggle with retrieving facts in certain categories as much as any of us do, and standardized tests were always his nemesis. But it took me one hour to teach him, at fifteen, to ride the bus alone. Ditto for many other daily life skills he wanted to learn.

In general terms, both of these young men could be called autistic. In its least damaging context, the word does little to meaningfully describe the unique challenges and needs each faces. "My child is "autistic" tells me nothing about him other than a broad-spectrum diagnosis. It doesn't help me understand his challenges, his strengths, his qualities both endearing and annoying. Who delights, puzzles or frightens him? What concerns, intrigues or uplifts him? We need to know these things, because in a more alarming context, the homogenous thinking a single-adjective descriptor engenders can prevent kids from getting the individualized services they need. That's the dichotomy, the fine line: in most cases, you need the label to be able to access the services. The label is not inaccurate or inherently bad. But it will be up to you to use it as a means of forward movement, not an excuse for you or others to use as a limiting factor.

We also need to beware the single-adjective descriptor that opens the door to its abuse. Around the world, many of us have seen numerous instances of "autistic" being used as general-purpose pejorative to describe a person who is uncooperative, belligerent, emotionally distant, or has difficulty communicating. I resist at every turn the usage of any language that robs our children of their right to be viewed, treated, and educated as individuals with specific needs and strengths. Cultural co-option of autism stereotypes as convenient slurs adds yet another barrier to society's acceptance of our children as whole persons, and another reason to steer our language toward more specific, more edifying representations of our children.

Many children with autism have grown and will grow into adults who choose to identify themselves as autistic; others will not ascribe to that label, or any other. In all cases, the choice is theirs alone. Ideally, they'll make it based on a childhood that began, as all childhoods should, with a blank slate of possibility. They arrive at adulthood after a moving staircase of years in which adults nurtured their skills and assets, provided education and guidance both cognitive and social-emotional, taught them informed self-advocacy and that their autism might be a reason behind some of their challenges, but never an excuse or free pass.

So whether autistic, with-autism, Aspie, autie, or spectrum dweller, run the word or words you use to describe your child through your reality-checker and ask yourself if it in any way limits your view of what the future holds for your child, and the value she or he brings to our world. If it does, remember that nothing, *nothing*, is predetermined and your time together brims with open-ended opportunity.

Chapter Two

My senses are out of sync.

This means that ordinary sights, sounds, smells, tastes, and touches you may not even notice can be very painful for me. What's going on around me often makes me uncomfortable, even scared. I may look like I'm spacing out or being mean to you, but it all feels like I have to defend myself. Here's why I may have trouble handling what you think is a simple trip to the grocery store:

My hearing may be hyperacute. I can hear dozens of people jabbering, even if they're far away, even if I can't see them. The loudspeaker booms today's special. Music blares from the sound system. Registers beep and cough, a coffee grinder chugs. The meat cutter screeches, babies wail, carts creak, the fluorescent lighting hums. My brain can't filter all the input and I'm in overload!

My sense of smell may be highly sensitive. The fish at the meat counter you don't seem to notice stinks to me, the guy standing next to us didn't take a shower today, the deli is handing out sausage samples, the baby in line ahead of us has a poopy diaper, they're mopping up a broken jar of pickles on aisle three with ammonia. I feel like throwing up.

And there's so much hitting my eyes! The fluorescent light is not only too bright, it flickers. The floor, the shelves, the stuff on the shelves—it all seems to be moving. The throbbing light bounces off everything and distorts what I'm seeing. There are too many items for me to be able to focus and parts of my brain may shut down.[1] There are whirling fans on the ceiling, so many strangers' faces and bodies moving all around me, coming so close it scares me. All this affects how I feel just standing there. And then it gets worse—I can't even feel where the edges of my body are. It's like I'm drifting in space.

1. In adult-speak, this coping response is what we might call "tunnel vision."

Sensory integration may be the most difficult aspect of autism to understand, but it might be the most critical. Our sensory systems are data gatherers; they're the "input" channels feeding information to our brains that help us figure out what's going on around us. Cognitive and social-emotional learning can't break through to a child whose world is intrusively loud, blindingly bright, unbearably malodorous and physically complicated to navigate. His brain can't filter multiple sensory inputs, and he frequently feels overloaded, disoriented, and unsettled in his own skin.

And into this shrieking, blinding hurricane of sensory acid rain we inject the expectation that this child "pay attention," "behave," learn, adhere to social rules that mystify her, and communicate with us, usually through a mode of our choosing, without thought about whether it's meaningful to her. Neglect a child's sensory challenges and you will never get close to discovering her capability. Sensory issues are that crucial to her overall ability to function.

Picture yourself on the world's hippest roller coaster. (If you dislike roller coasters, this makes the example even better.) Coney Island and Six Flags are fun vacation venues, but how long could you do your day job while ensconced on the Wonder Woman Golden Lasso, Steel Vengeance, or the Kingda Ka? Could you conduct that meeting, teach that class, be charming dinner company, write the report and clean the house while enduring the vertigo, the screams of fellow riders, the g-force of the rushing air, the

Neglect a child's sensory challenges and you will never get close to discovering her capability.

unexpected drops and abrupt changes of direction, the sensation of hair in your mouth and bugs in your teeth? It might be fun as an occasional thrill, but admit it—you want to get off after the three-minute ride. For many autistic children, it's a ride with no exit gate, a 24/7 state of being, and the very antithesis of thrilling.

It's natural that we shy away from concepts and conditions that demand arduous effort to comprehend, that we seek easier solutions. For the nonprofessional, gaining a working understanding of how sensory processing issues affect a particular child can be downright intimidating. An area of immense complexity, it pervades everything we do or try to do. That's why it's the first outpost of autism we should address.

Science has long recognized that sensory integration takes place in the brainstem, and that sensory processing dysfunction causes what amounts to a traffic pile-up in the brain. You may already be looking right at the manifestation of sensory overload and not recognize it. Hands over the ears is an obvious indication. Less obvious but no less compelling are the behaviors you'll often see referred to as stims, self-stimulating conduct such as rocking, chewing, flapping, rubbing, wandering, and other repetitive mannerisms. Seemingly inexplicable behavior such as aggression, excessive silliness, clumsiness, and over- or underreaction to injury can have an underlying sensory cause. In the case of more extreme behavior such as meltdowns, the trigger may not be obvious; nevertheless, sensory overload should be the first suspect brought in for questioning. That questioning can be tricky, intricate, and protracted. But one of the few universal truths about autism is this: no matter how unprovoked, how random it may appear, behavior never, ever comes out of nowhere. There is always a trigger (and we will discuss this at length in Chapter Nine). Find it you must, and keep in mind that if your child is nonspeaking, has limited vocabulary and/or no alternate functional means of communicating with you, she won't be able to tell you what's causing such discomfort. Even your chatterbox child with Asperger's, who seems so verbally competent, may not have the vocabulary or self-awareness sophisticated enough to describe what's happening within her complicated neurology.

Developing a practical understanding of sensory integration can be challenging. As many as twenty-one sensory systems are at work in our bodies. You're familiar with the predominant five: visual (sight), auditory (sound), tactile (touch), olfactory (smell), and gustatory (taste). Four other senses are commonly attributed to humans:

1. Equilibrioception: sense of balance or vestibular sense

2. Proprioception and kinesthesia: orientation and motion of one's limbs and body in space

3. Nocioception: pain, three kinds: cutaneous/superficial, somatic/deep tissue or muscle, visceral/organs

4. Interoception: helps us regulate our body's internal state— tired, hungry, need to eliminate, physical manifestations of anxiety such as heart or breathing rate.

When any of these senses fall out of calibration, they can wreak havoc in your child's life.

Comprehensive discussion of the sensory systems is beyond the scope of this chapter. What follows here is a short description of seven primary senses and what their dysfunction can mean for the child with autism. Hyperacute sensory systems call for calming overloaded senses. But senses can also be hypoacute, or underresponsive. The need in those cases is to alert, not calm, the underresponding sense. An occupational therapist well-versed in autism can be invaluable in evaluating, explaining and addressing your child or student's individual issues. Bear in mind, too, that acuity may not be the same across all the child's senses. Some may be hyper, some may be hypo, and some can vary day to day, even hour to hour.

The visual sense

For many children with autism, the visual sense is their strongest. The good news/bad news is that while they rely more heavily on visual input to learn and navigate their world, it can be the first sense to become overstimulated. Bright lights or objects, reflective surfaces, too many objects in the field of vision or objects moving at fast or irregular speeds can cause distortion and sensory chaos. So pervasive is this sense for many autistic children that it warrants its own chapter later in the book.

We'll note here though that while the visual sense may be the most robust in many children with autism, there will be some for whom the visual sense is underactive or disorganized. This may manifest itself in a child who sways or rocks (attempting to change angle of visual perspective), is leery of changes in elevation (ladders, stairs), or becomes fascinated with moving objects (model trains, water wheels). Physical limitations may also be in play. Some children may lack depth perception, have limited fields of vision (think of looking through a paper towel tube and missing everything else around you), or the visual picture of their world may look distorted and fragmented, like a Picasso painting.

The auditory sense

Our auditory sense provides us with a tremendous amount of information. We take in and instantly interpret the component qualities of sound—volume, pitch, frequency, vibration—and the directionality of it. We turn our head to seek out voices, footsteps, and traffic. When hearing is typically calibrated, we perk up and attend to whispers to glean what's being said, and only the loudest sounds will cause us to recoil, cover our ears, or otherwise protect ourselves.

For many autistic individuals, the auditory sense is the most commonly impaired. Hyperacute hearing can cause agonizing pain. The sounds of an average day are too loud, too high-pitched, too sudden, too sharp, too intrusive. An autistic child may hear things undetectable to your ear, escalating an already overwhelming world into deafening dissonance. She likely lacks the ability to suppress and/or filter sound, to distinguish your voice over the sound of the dryer or the television, or the teacher's voice over the murmurs and movements of others in the classroom. Environments that appear orderly to the casual observer may be a confusing minefield of clatter for the child with auditory hypersensitivity.

Obvious too-loud flags like blaring music, gymnasium basketball, cafeteria and playground cacophony, and emergency vehicle sirens are examples of everyday commotion that can induce physical pain. Sudden loud sounds such as fire drills or cars backfiring can trigger a level of panic from which your child may take hours to recover. In extreme examples, the child has been able to hear the heartbeats of others in the room. As for enjoying the pounding surf at the beach, forget surf. Think pounding, as in headache.

Less apparent but as invasive or intolerable are ordinary, seemingly nonthreatening noises. He's not hiding in his room because he doesn't like his family; he's fleeing the dissonance of the dishwasher, coffeemaker, washer, dryer, leaf blower, and television all having their say at once. He might as well be right inside that spin cycle himself. Over at school, his peers in the classroom listen as the teacher speaks. But the child with autism cannot identify the voice of the teacher as the primary sound to which he should be attuned. To him it's indistinguishable from the grinding of the pencil sharpener, the fly buzzing on the windowsill, the lawn mower chugging outside, the child with the constant cough behind him, and the class next door tromping down the hall to the library.

Well-known author and autism advocate Dr. Temple Grandin, who writes and speaks extensively about her own experiences as an autistic person, puts this succinct grace note on it: "Wal-Mart is like being inside the speaker at a rock concert."

And a friendly warning: your child's hyperacute hearing isn't always painful, and may lean toward comic book superhero or Dr. Seuss territory. Many of us remember Dr. Seuss' story *The Big Brag*, with its rabbit who claimed he could hear a fly cough ninety miles away. Extreme example, extreme fun. But it's not unusual for an autistic child to be able to hear—and repeat—conversations that took place across a room or outdoor space, behind windows or doors. One mom swore to me (facetiously) that her daughter could hear a potato chip bag opening in the next county. My toddler son often looked at the sky and said "airplane" thirty seconds before I could hear or see it. Your child's hyperacute hearing may give new meaning to the old idiom, "Little pitchers have big ears."

Hypoacute (undersensitive) hearing brings its own brand of trouble. It impacts language development and use, social-emotional learning, and academics. Children may miss pieces of what's being said, be unable to process certain types of sounds, or may perceive what they hear as long strings of sounds rather than individual words and phrases. What looks like laziness or noncompliance may be a sensory impairment that prevents them from capturing and/or processing the ordinary sounds of daily life.

The child with an understimulated auditory sense also struggles to process information coming from sound. He may speak too softly or too loudly, seek out noisy appliances (lawn mowers, hair dryers, blenders), or environments for additional sensory input, handle toys and other objects roughly to create crashing noises, exhibit fascination with rushing water (waterfalls, running bathwater, flushing toilets), or like vibrating/buzzing toys.

Whether over- or understimulated, suspect auditory processing difficulties if your child or student can follow written or visual directives well, but struggles with or is unable to comprehend oral instruction.

The tactile sense

Our skin registers an astonishing amount of information: light touches as well as deeper pressure, a wide range of temperatures, different types of pain or irritation, vibration and other movement, and textures ranging from slimy to rough.

Hypersensitivity to touch is called tactile defensiveness. An autistic child, trapped in her own skin, is unable to regulate distressing sensations that rain upon her in the form of uncomfortable clothes, unwelcome touches from other people (hugs that might seem warm and friendly to you might be torture to her) and unpleasant textures of things she's confronted with touching or eating.

For the tactile-defensive child, clothing tags, buttons, zippers, elastic around wrists or necks, and similar clothing embellishments cause constant distraction. Whether indoors or out, going barefoot is not an option (do you have a tip toe walker in your house?). The child may evade your embrace, and fight like a badger against haircuts, shampooing, teeth brushing, and nail clipping. Hands-on tasks like finger painting and sand table activities may induce more stress than fun.

Hyposensitivity results in understimulation and a child who craves tactile sensation. She's the child who runs her hand along the wall walking from class to class, must touch everyone and everything, or may not be affected by temperature shifts. She may exhibit perplexing, even disturbing behavior, sometimes bordering on danger. She may stim to the point of hurting herself (biting, pinching, applying pressure with various objects, brushing teeth too hard), unaware of the intensity of her actions and her high threshold to pain and temperature. She may prefer tight, heavy, or textured clothing, or engage in odd activities such as taking a bath fully clothed. She may purposely touch or bump into objects and other people to enliven her senses, then eventually shy away from trying new motor activities after others react to her "clumsiness" with impatience, irritation or mockery. Because children with hypotactile processing seek constant contact, parents may characterize them as clingy and others may find their touches invasive and inappropriate.

Most occupational therapists will tell you how successful they can be at desensitizing a hyperacute tactile sense or awakening a hypoacute sense. Take it as true from a mom whose child spent the early years of his life sporting only his birthday suit whenever he could get away with it and doling out backwards hugs (facing away) to a precious few. By third grade he chose jeans and flannel shirts. By fifth grade he had hiked, biked, backpacked, and white-watered the Great Outdoors with all kinds of slimy-crawly critters and substances without batting an eye. That's what's possible with appropriate and regular intervention.

The olfactory sense

"Ewwwww, what stinks?" was a common refrain in our household, often when my nose detected nothing. Paraeducators tell me that their autistic students greet them with "You smell funny!" though they're fresh from the shower. Olfactory defensiveness (hyperacute sense of smell) is common among autistic children. Aromas, scents, and fragrances the typical population regards as pleasant or undetectable have the power to make the child with autism miserable, even ill. If a certain paint, glue, perfume, or floor cleaner has ever given you an instant headache, if the smell of fish, broccoli, garlic, cat food, or limburger cheese has ever turned your stomach or brought tears to your eyes, multiply that sensation many times over and you'll get an inkling of what your child may be experiencing. Don't ask your child to change the kitty litter box. That "odor free"/natural citrus/recycled pine concoction, combined with the you-know-what that lurks within, will knock the poor kid back into yesterday.

Here are potential olfactory offenders in the home:

- scented laundry products (if it's on his clothes, he can't get away from it)
- scented soaps, body washes, and shampoos (includes kid scents, such as bubble gum)
- bathroom air fresheners (they only add another layer of odor)
- hand, face and body lotions
- deodorants, aftershaves, colognes
- hair styling products
- nail products

- housecleaning products such as ammonia, bleach, furniture polish, carpet cleaning solution, wet wipes, other fragranced cleaners

- cooking odors

- yard and garden chemicals

In the school setting, we have the art area, odiferous science projects, classmates' body washes and shampoos, scented pens, the old oil-burning furnace or the window that opens onto the newly-mowed, composting lawn, the hamster cage and the days-old forgotten lunch in the closet. More than one student with autism has been known to experience the uncontrollable gag reflex in the cafeteria. (Offer an alternative place to eat lunch if lunchtime smells disturb your student.)

An understimulated olfactory sense shows itself in a child who may seem overinterested in sniffing her own body and others, or conversely, doesn't smell her own body odor and therefore might not realize when bathing or oral care is needed. She may put unusual nonfood items in her mouth such as dirt, paste, coins, or soap, or she may exhibit lack of sensitivity to odors others consider offensive, such as urine (bedwetting) and feces (smearing). Both of the foregoing can also be signs of an understimulated tactile sense.

The gustatory sense

Our sense of taste ties closely to the olfactory sense. The olfactory sense acts as a kind of sentry. If a potential food item smells dangerous—moldy, burnt, rancid, or otherwise "off"—we don't put it in our mouths. It's nature's way of protecting us from ingesting poisons and toxins. A person's olfactory sensations can alter how an individual perceives the flavor of a substance. A hyperacute gustatory system reacts with increased sensitivity to pungent tastes like bitterness (such as the phytochemicals found in many vegetables) and heat (spicy foods containing capsaicin, such as chili). It may also reject foods based on temperature or texture; the child may shun cold foods (ice cream or refrigerated juice), oozy/slippery foods (puddings, canned peaches, condiments), or mixed-consistency foods, such as casseroles, sandwiches, or soups. The grainy texture of meat frequently offends, as may carbonated drinks. The result is that many children with ASD are selective eaters to a breathtaking degree, sometimes limiting themselves to only a few foods.

On the other end of the sensitivity scale is the hypotaster. This child may have a reduced perception of taste, and may 1) eat everything in sight because it all tastes good, 2) eat little because food as a pleasant sensory experience has no meaning or interest, 3) eat unusual taste combinations of food (e.g., French fries dipped in peach yogurt, peanut butter on a hot dog), or 4) eat a horrifying array of nonfood items, like dirt, clay, glue, coffee grounds, dust bunnies, and paper.

Underlying physiological problems, such as mineral deficiencies, can also alter a child's sense of taste and can result in poor oral hygiene, which also can lead to viral or bacterial infections.

The health implications for both hypertasters (sometimes called supertasters) and hypotasters are troubling. The hypertasters reject many of the foods providing the highest health benefits, like vegetables. The hypotasters are susceptible to just the opposite, the excesses of oral gratification and illnesses associated with overeating and, later in their adult life, possibly alcohol and smoking.

Addressing gustatory sensitivities requires an educated eye, a fine-tuned assessment, as well as time and patience. For the sake of your own sanity, "don't try this at home" without the advice of an occupational therapist.

The vestibular and proprioceptive senses

Like a well-run corporate accounting office, these two critical but little understood senses get no attention when everything is running smoothly. Only when things go awry do we become aware of the mayhem created when an essential piece of infrastructure malfunctions.

The vestibular system regulates the sense of equilibrium (balance, stability) by responding to changes in the position of the eyes and head. Its command center is located in the inner ear. The proprioceptive sense uses feedback from joints and muscles to tell us where our body is in space and what forces and pressures are acting upon it. Because vestibular and proprioceptive problems are not easily recognized by the untrained eye, they often go unidentified and untreated, leaving the autistic child to cope unaided within a very hostile environment.

Impairments to the vestibular and proprioceptive senses can hamper or halt everyday motor functions. The child may trip over his own feet, bounce off walls, and fall out of chairs. He may experience gravitational insecurity, becoming anxious in settings that take his feet off solid ground, such as climbing the steps to the slide, using a public toilet, riding a bike and sitting on a too-tall chair or stool without a footrest. We may unwittingly add to his anxieties about managing fundamental movements with our additional expectation that he learn new skills, whether cognitive/academic, social, or gross motor. In this regard, it's easy to understand why many children with ASD shy away from sports, with their overwhelming multiple expectations: assume certain positions, have the gross motor skills and motor planning ability to execute sequential moves such as diving for the ball, catching it, jumping up and throwing it, or to dribble, aim, and shoot a basketball. Then add in the social cognitive elements: remember the rules, apply the rules, communicate with teammates, and accept the fallout when you blow a play.

Vestibular disorder can affect nearly every function of the body, causing a dizzying (literally) range of symptoms including, but not limited to, loss of balance, chronic nausea, distorted hearing (ears may feel stuffed, or sound may come across as full of static, like bad radio reception), and visual disturbances (objects or printed material appears to be blurry or in motion). Distance focus may be difficult, glare from lights may seem exaggerated, and the child may have difficulty with memory and/or focus, chronic fatigue, acute anxiety, and depression.

Children with proprioceptive dysfunction may walk with an odd, heavy gait, have trouble with tableware, pencils, and other fine motor implements, lose their balance when their eyes are closed, or be "crashers," forever running into or jumping off things as they seek deep pressure sensory input. They may be "space invaders" who, not understanding the multi-faceted concept of personal distance (proxemic communication, discussed in Chapter Eight), continually and unwittingly get too close to others, often unintentionally or involuntarily bumping into them.

In addition to that invaluable occupational therapist, an adapted physical education (APE) specialist can help with large motor issues, modifying curriculum and equipment so your child can participate with his peers in PE and playground activities. Ask if your school district has a special education motor team or APE consultant.

25

Concerted effort

Most children on the autism spectrum struggle with more than one sensory challenge. The type and extent of the differences (hyper in one, hypo in another, or any combination) can shift and change, day to day, over time, and with treatment. "Concerted" has two meanings—strenuous, and collaborative. To alleviate the very authentic sensory challenges our children face, they need from us concerted effort in both its definitions: team tactics, with parents, school, and therapist all working together.

One of the occupational therapist's most effective tools is a child-specific plan of action called the sensory diet, sometimes called a sensory map. A sensory diet or map identifies a child's particular sensory needs and prescribes regularly scheduled activities that help him organize sensory input in a manner that makes it easier to attend, engage, and self-regulate. Through formal and informal observation and evaluation, your OT will determine three components:

1. The child's level of sensory arousal as it fluctuates throughout the day. Low arousal/hyposensitivity requires alerting inputs. Over arousal/hypersensitivity requires calming inputs.

2. Current state of the child's sensory systems (which senses are strong, and which are challenged).

3. Documentation to determine the source of the sensory challenge, of specific incidents that set off emotional or behavioral responses (transitions, certain activities, locations or people, having to deal with certain substances).

A primary goal of sensory therapy is to help the child learn to self-recognize sensory issues as they arise and then use the strategies we teach them to self-regulate or request them to self-regulate or request help when that isn't possible. These might include regularly scheduled movement breaks, providing fidget or chew toys, and making a study carrel or quiet corner available. Embedding strategies into his day activities that both address his needs and play to his strengths will give him a sense of control and can-do that heightens his ability to engage both cognitively and socially.

Sensory processing dysfunction isn't exclusive to autism, and it may help you understand your child's needs if you reflect upon your own sensory sensitivities and those of the people around you. In Carol Kranowitz's lighthearted but revealing children's book *The Goodenoughs Get in Sync*, every family member right down to the dog works to cope with a different set of sensory processing difficulties. Dad can't tell the difference between grape and strawberry jellies, nor can he judge which of two shovels is heavier. Mom must always be "touching things, moving around, stretching, humming, chewing, fiddling with pencil, chalk or rubber band." The children describe their struggles with fight-flight-freeze response, their difficulty articulating, their gravitational insecurity, visual defensiveness, audio discrimination, dyspraxia, and other motor-based difficulties. When the family members ignore their sensory needs, the household descends into chaos. But when they resume their sensory-diet activities, equilibrium returns. Each tells his or her own story and as you might guess, the children's voices are riveting.

Forget the Pyramid of Giza and the Hanging Gardens of Babylon, the real Wonders of the World are the neurological senses whose function or dysfunction hold such profound power over us. Seven years of devoted sensory training helped my wordless, aggressive toddler grow into a confident, capable and kind-hearted teen able to self-manage his sensory needs. Now that's a monument.

Chapter Three

See the difference between won't (I choose
not to) and can't (I'm not able to).

You may think I don't listen to instructions, or I just don't want to do what you ask. But that's not the reason I don't comply. It's that I can't understand you, or I'm not sure what to do. Like when you call to me from across the room, I hear "*ξ^%$#@, Jordan. #$%^*ξ^%$ξ*." Instead, come over to me, get my attention, and speak in plain words: "Jordan, put your book in your desk. It's time to go to lunch." This tells me what you want me to do and what is going to happen next. Now I can do it.

Sometimes what you're asking me to do hurts, or makes me uncomfortable, and I don't know how to control it.

Sometimes I don't know how to tell you why I can't.
But I know it's not because I don't want to. It's because
I'm not able to.

Is a zebra white with black stripes or black with white stripes? Ask ten people or pull up ten websites and you'll get twelve opinions. Zebras give the impression of being white with black stripes because the stripes end without joining under the belly and around the legs. But the hide of the zebra is actually black. It's a lesson from Mother Nature that things are not always as they appear on the surface.

And so it is with many of the complexities of autism. How do we distinguish between what our child won't do (chooses not to, behavior based on temperament or personality, or patterns acquired through upbringing, etc.) and what he can't do (is not able to)? Many "won't" allegations about our kids are behavior complaints. He won't comply; she won't listen to instructions; he won't stop rapping his knuckles; she walks away in mid-sentence, or other odd, seemingly inexplicable or narrowly-focused actions. We adults assume comprehension (functional and social), assume that because he did something once, he can repeat the behavior without further prompting, practice, or reinforcement, under all circumstances. As adults do with so many challenges our children face, we make all sorts of assumptions about knowledge and ability without stopping to consider that our assumptions may be the root of the problem at hand.

"Won't" and "can't" aren't interchangeable. "Won't," the contraction of "will not," implies premeditation, intent, and deliberate behavior. It involves having both the self-awareness and developmental readiness to consider the situation, possible consequences, and make a decision. "Can't," the contraction of "cannot," acknowledges that a behavior isn't a matter of choice, but is rooted in lack of ability, knowledge, or opportunity.

The distinction between "can't" and "won't" is clear-cut, because where behavior is concerned, there are two absolutes.

All behavior is communication.

All behavior happens for a reason.

Today's psychology recognizes varied motives for behavior: bids for attention, sensory seeking or sensory avoidance, feelings of power-lessness, testing boundaries, experimentation at different stages of cognitive and social development, explorations into independence, and many others. Some may be the direct result of challenges arising from autism; others may be developmental stages that all children, autism or not, pass through. The next time you catch yourself saying, "He won't..." stop and evaluate your child's behavior in light of the following more common reasons. See if you start recognizing situations where "can't" is a more accurate description than "won't."

Resistant/avoidant behavior. Your child or student doesn't know how to do what you've asked or it's unpleasant to him for a reason you don't perceive.

It's natural for a child (or adult) to want to evade an unpleasant task. Pinpointing the source of the resistance is necessary to resolving it. Your essential role is now behavior detective. You may be surprised at how often lack of ability, information, or opportunity plays into your child's or student's reluctance or refusal to do what you've asked; think "close to 100% of the time." Possible reasons (get coffee; we'll be here a while):

- He didn't hear your request or only pieces filtered through to his brain.

- He doesn't comprehend the instructions or the request.

- He doesn't know or understand the rules, the process, or the routine.

- He doesn't have the fine or gross motor skills to accomplish the task.

- The behavioral or academic expectation is too high.

- The activity is sensory-overwhelming.

- The task causes physical discomfort.

- The request comes at a time when he's hungry or too tired to comply.

- Any of the above, alone or combined, causes disabling anxiety.

In other words, he can't.

On top of that, he dreads failure and criticism. In his concrete, black-and-white, all-or-nothing perspective, errors and successes come in two sizes: huge or nonexistent. This breeds pervasive stress and anxiety in him. Further, have you offered choice or flexibility in how and when he must accomplish the task? Has he had any say in how he could best tackle it? Avoidance behaviors frequently stem from lack of comprehension and fear of failure.

Allowing her a say in how to best accomplish tasks and assignments betters her chance of success, which in turn motivates her to try and do the real work involved. Ask, probe, and guide: how might she be better able to accomplish a task or meet an expectation? Help her finish the sentence: "It would be better if _____."

- An adult helped me.

- A peer or sibling helped me.

- I had more time.

- I could work by myself.

- I could do it with a partner or group.

- I could work in a different place.

- I could show you or tell you in another way. I could:

  ○ Tell you about it, in private or in a small group.

  ○ Write about it.

  ○ Draw, paint or show you with toys or manipulatives.

  ○ Type or record my thoughts about it on a tablet or computer.

  ○ Show you on the computer or tablet another way.

Attention-seeking behavior. Your child wants adult or peer attention.

The good news is, he wants to interact. The bad news is that inappropriate attention-seeking behavior frequently disrupts classrooms and family routine. If you're exasperated because he "won't" stop, consider: has he been taught, and does he understand how to ask for attention or help in an appropriate manner? It's one of autism's nasty Catch 22s that the child must be carefully taught about social interaction, but at the same time lacks the understanding of when and how to ask for help. He needs specific instruction and examples to make requests such as "I need help" or "I don't understand this," and he needs emotional bolstering while he learns to summon not just the appropriate words or actions, but the courage to ask.

Also consider whether or not he gets sufficient adult attention to achieve what's expected of him. Similarly, does he receive adequate and appropriate attention from peers to validate his self-worth? Does he draw more attention from you for his undesirable deeds than he does for the more suitable behaviors? Is the amount of praise he hears from you greater than the amount of complaining? (A 5:1 praise-criticism ratio is widely advocated by educators and psychologists.) Do you unknowingly reinforce the behaviors you want to quell? If you ignore her when she's not being disruptive but take immediate notice when the spitballs sail or she uses the sofa as a trampoline, she's gotten the attention she wanted, and you've reinforced her inappropriate behaviors. Remember our maxim: all behavior is communication. It applies to you, too.

Self-calming. As we discussed in Chapter Two, your child unconsciously attempts to calm or alert over- or understimulated senses to reduce anxiety or discomfort. This may be the underlying organic cause of a behavior, and until we help the child learn sensory strategies he's able to use, such behavior falls into the "I can't" category. Please notice that I said "help the child learn strategies he's able to use" rather than "teach the child." It isn't teaching

> **It isn't teaching if he didn't learn it, and it's not learning if he's not able to make use of the information.**

if he didn't learn it, and it's not learning if he's not able to make use of the information. As you'll hear often throughout this book (like our kids, we don't always learn something at the first exposure), opening the channel between teaching and learning often requires a mode other than what might be your first choice.

Entertainment/fun. Your child finds a particular behavior amusing to himself.

While children with ASD often have a more rigid or reduced sense of play than typical kids, they can also be resourceful at entertaining themselves. It's a grand skill, as any mother of an "I'm bored. There's nothing to do" kid will tell you. However, being able to interact effectively in a group is an essential life skill. Early play skills should develop in a manner that leads to being able to handle group work at school, maneuver cliques during adolescence, and be effective team players as adults in the workplace, in community involvement, in recreational pursuits.) If your child repeats the diverting behaviors when others aren't present, it may be his way of telling you he wants to play but has neither adequate skill nor the opportunity to interact with other children.

Play skills develop along a timeline progressing from solitary play to being an observer of others at play, then on to parallel play and finally cooperative play. By identifying where your child falls on this developmental timeline, you and your child's team can set up a plan that can be implemented consistently between home and school. Like all such plans, it will evolve over time as your child's group skills expand and progress.

Control. Your child is trying to order or reorder his environment.

When so little is within their control, many children on the autism spectrum experience life as a continuous battle to hold onto whatever power they do have to keep order and consistency in their lives. Their attempts to control may be overt (confrontational, aggressive behavior that looks like defiance), or they may be passive-aggressive (they silently or covertly continue to do what feels right or comfortable regardless of attempts at redirecting behavior).

Your daily life as a typical adult flows in a perpetual, minute by-minute stream of choices. You take for granted both the array of choices you have and your ability to act upon them. Such reasoning and decision-making skills are much more limited in your autistic child. What appears to be controlling behavior on your child's part can also be seen as evidence of her ability to think independently and affirm her own wants and needs. Channel these qualities as you work with her to instill decision-making skills and increase the number of choices and opportunities for success in her world.

It's too easy to get into a power struggle with a child who seems hell-bent on having things his way, but always remind yourself of your goals for this child before you respond. Is your goal to bend the child to your will, make him respect your authority, and force his compliance at all costs? (Ask yourself if that really is a win.) Or is the goal to acclimate him to socially acceptable behavior in a manner that enables him to grow as a person and take his place as a citizen of the world?

As a young child, Bryce had a passive-aggressive manner of letting us know when he had had enough of a social situation: he would tell us—once. If we did not end the outing within a timeframe reasonable to him (less than five minutes), he would simply turn and go. Depending upon where we were, you can imagine how dangerous this could be. I still break out in hives remembering those times, his little back disappearing down the street or into the crowd. We quickly learned that when Bryce said, "I'm ready to go," that meant nonnegotiable departure time. Was he pulling our strings? Were we letting him run the show? Not by a long shot. He was telling us that he was approaching his meltdown point. This was an enormous developmental achievement in self-awareness and self-advocacy, a milestone reached through the devoted efforts and guidance of parents, therapists, and teachers. It demanded and deserved our respect. We ungrudgingly adapted our plans accordingly. Our goal was that Bryce be able to handle and enjoy social settings in a manner that would allow us to do things as an entire family. To accomplish that goal, we had to learn to listen and heed his verbal and nonverbal warnings when he reached the limits of his current abilities. We beat numerous hasty retreats in those days, but over time Bryce gained language, confidence, sensory tolerance, and social skills. We did it his way, and by his teens, we had a go-anywhere young man who got around town on his own and, to celebrate his high school graduation, traveled across the country solo.

Retribution. Your child wants to retaliate for treatment perceived as unfair.

I include this one here because it's most likely a motivation you can rule out.

"He's doing it to get back at me." Let it go, my friend. The concept of fair/unfair, being able to take the perspective of others, consider their thoughts, feelings, intentions and motivations, is highly complex at the social processing level and something many children with autism notoriously lack. What's more, planning and carrying out revenge requires advanced executive skills coupled with a level of motor planning beyond the abilities of most children on the spectrum. Keep looking. Your answer isn't here.

Once we understand how "can't" shapes our child's behavior, we must turn the word on ourselves, because "can't" is a two-faced monster. "Can't" comes in two flavors, and it sits on a very different place on the tongue when "can't" comes from you rather than your child. You, as a capable adult, don't get off the hook as easily with "can't." As we've defined it, "can't" reflects lack of knowledge, ability, and opportunity. I'm the first to acknowledge that autism demands a huge learning curve, but we're talking at a deeper level here, about playing the hand you've been dealt. It's not about backing away from difficulty and challenge in the face of your own insecurities. You didn't get a choice about the nature part of your child, but the nurture part grants you choices without number. Your child will be an expression of his personality and environment. What vibe does he get from you? Are you a can-do adult?

See the difference between won't and can't.

Some years ago, I met a parent who could not break free of his anti-government rant about how, by mandating vaccines for school attendance, he had been robbed of his son. "I simply can't relate to him," he sighed. "How do you think it feels to know that he'll probably end up in jail?" It's a scary, helpless feeling to be weighed down by regrets and broken dreams. But this parent had crossed the line from can't (am not able to) into won't (I choose not to) with the decision to look only backward into what-might-have-been, rather than forward into possibilities yet unexplored. Regardless of whether a vaccination is liable for his son's condition—and I won't (choose not to) debate that subject—it's an after-the-fact discussion. The child can't (proper use of the word here) be un-vaccinated. By adopting a defeatist attitude rather than the more work-intensive proactive approach to help his child achieve his full potential, this parent also chose paralysis, fear, exasperation, and self-fulfilling prophecy. His son was eight years old, a bright, articulate, clever, and resourceful child. He was also aggressive, angry, and frustrated—like Dad. A lifetime of "can't" messages can plant the germ of despair in a child.

I suggested to this parent that he try to reframe "can't." Your son can't change that he has autism. He can't find his way to something better unless the adults around him step up to help.

I told this parent that I knew him to be more capable and caring than that. And I asked him, as my pediatrician used to ask me, who is the adult here? Who has the power to change things? Can you? With help and education, you can be the teacher and guide in your child's life. Will you? He had yet to answer that question for himself.

The irony and the poignancy of can't vs. won't is that we adults often kill the very thing we want most dearly to achieve. If you yearn for a confident, optimistic, curious and engaged child, you must model those qualities and you must find and reinforce them in your child, however tiny the increment of gain. Think carefully about the role of reinforcement in your relationship with your child or student. The nuances may be subtle, but the manner in which you respond to your child's actions, words, or attitude amounts to either affirmation or denigration. Watch what you reinforce; be sure it's something you want him or her to repeat. When you take on a can-do attitude, he can-do, too.

If you find yourself governed by thoughts such as, I can't give this child special treatment, I can't put extra time into modifying tasks, assignments or environments, and I can't do anything about the way this kid is, then you can't expect to see positive changes. Thoughtfully constructing the child's world in a manner that ensures a flow of successes, however bite-sized they may be, builds a foundation that buries the won'ts beneath it. That's not special treatment. It's respecting and teaching to the strengths and challenges of a child who experiences the world and learns through channels that may differ from yours, and that may step outside what you assume from so-called typical kids. It's guiding him through the skill-building that will help him grow to be as independent as he possibly can. It's what we like to think of as "the right way" within the lens of "for this child."

Think back to those days before you had a child.

You went to a bar after work and called it Happy Hour or Attitude Adjustment Hour. You had a goal: to make your world more pleasant, more palatable, or to ease the day's challenges. This isn't much different. You choose to make a conscious shift in your mental state, this time for your child. If you don't like the boozy connotation, think of it as energy resource management: how much time and energy do you expend dwelling on what you don't have and can't have because of your child's autism? That's called

40

brooding. How much could you accomplish if you redirected that energy into doing, trying, and reaching forward? That's called progress—for you both.

Chapter Four

I'm a concrete thinker.
I interpret language literally.

You confuse me by saying, "Hold your horses, cowboy!" when what you mean is, "Stop running." Don't tell me something is "a piece of cake" when there's no dessert in sight and what you mean is, "This will be easy to do."

When you say, "It's very cold outside," I think you're stating a fact. I don't understand that you mean, "Wear long pants today, not shorts."

Don't say, "Let's wrap this up," when there's no gift around and what you mean is to finish what I'm doing.

And when you say, "it's just an expression"—that makes no sense to me.

All the different ways people talk can be baffling to me. If you teach me, I can and will learn what some of these crazy phrases mean. But for now, I need you to tell me plainly what you want me to do, and what exactly you're trying to say about what's going on around us.

Whatever command of your native language you thought you had will be seriously tested by your literal minded child or student with autism. Many idioms, puns, nuances, inferences, metaphors, allusions, and sarcasm that make up a startling amount of our conversation are lost on him. You'll be taken at your word to a degree you've never had to confront before. British Olympic medalist Doug Larson sums up the pitfalls of colloquial communication with the woeful assertion, "If the English language made any sense, a catastrophe would be an apostrophe with fur."

To autistic children, with their concrete, visual thinking, their (sometimes brilliant) associative abilities and, for many, their limited vocabularies, the imagery generated by common idioms and other figures of speech must be very disturbing. Ants in his pants? Butterflies in her stomach? Open a can of worms? Cat got your tongue?

It's enough to make them want to drive the porcelain bus. (Like that one? It means throw up—er—vomit.)

That imagery they conjure is at the root of some of our everyday expressions. When you tell him it's raining cats and dogs, you mean it's raining hard. One interpretation of the origin of this idiom goes back to the English floods of the seventeenth and eighteenth centuries. After torrential downpours, the bodies of drowned cats and dogs littered the streets. It appeared as if they had rained from the skies.

And I'm sure this is what many young ones with autism visualize when you say it's raining cats and dogs. "I don't see them!" fretted one little boy. "It only looks like falling-down water!" while another watched a cloudburst and surmised, "They must all be on the ground already." Heaven help you if he hears you telling someone it's a dog-eat-dog world, that you toasted the bride and groom, or that you warned someone not to throw the baby out with the bathwater.

You wouldn't dream of issuing instructions to your child in a foreign language, but English can seem that way. A popular Internet essay notes: "There is no egg in eggplant, neither apple nor pine in pineapple. A guinea pig is neither from Guinea nor is it a pig. If the plural of tooth is teeth, why isn't the plural of booth beeth? One goose, two geese. So one moose, two meese? If teachers taught, why haven't preachers praught? We have noses that run and feet that smell. How can a slim chance and a fat chance be the same, while a wise man and a wise guy are opposites?"

> **You wouldn't dream of issuing instructions to your child in a foreign language, but English can seem that way.**

The lunacy continues with homographs. The nurse wound gauze around the wound. Farms produce produce. The birds scattered, and the dove dove into the woods. When you get close to the window, close it. Lead me to the lead pipe. Go polish the Polish table. Can you wind your watch in the wind?

Communicating with a literal-thinking child requires that we pause to consider our phrasing. It may take some retraining—yours. In time, with maturity and education, the concrete-thinking child can acclimate to some degree of recognizing idioms and other figurative language. While he's young and his receptive language challenges are many, don't add to his befuddlement. Watch for common snags like these:

Idioms and clichés

Don't say:	Instead say:
You're the apple of my eye.	I love you very much.
I'm at the end of my rope.	I'm getting angry.
Bite your tongue.	Don't speak to me like that.
Let's call it a day.	It's time to stop for now.
I smell a rat.	This doesn't seem right to me.

Nonspecific instructions

Say exactly what you mean and don't make your child or student figure out nonspecific instructions.

Don't say:	Instead say:
Hang it over there.	Hang your coat on the hook by the door.
Stay out of the street.	Stop your bike at the end of the driveway.
Quit kicking.	Keep your feet under your desk.
Let's get going.	We're going home now.

Inferences

Similar to the nonspecific instruction, an inference comes across to the autistic child as merely a statement of fact. Don't make him guess. Specify the action you want him to take.

Don't say:	Instead say:
Your room's a mess.	Hang up your clothes.
You didn't turn your homework in.	Put your book report on my desk.
I don't like that noise.	Turn down the sound on the TV.

Phrasal Verbs

Phrasal verbs combine a verb with a preposition or adverb to form common expressions that can be as confusing as idioms to the concrete thinker.

Don't say:	Instead say:
We look up to him.	We admire him; he sets a good example.
The car is acting up.	The car (or part of the car) is not working right.
Jamie got kicked out of class.	The teacher sent Jamie to talk with the principal.

We read, hear and talk a great deal about "autism awareness." This is one area where our own awareness often needs a jump-start, or periodic reminder. Figurative language is pervasive and deeply embedded in our verbal communication. In addition to the examples I've already given, it includes allusion ("he's a regular Einstein!"), hyperbole ("I'm gonna sleep for a year"), irony ("as friendly as a wolverine"), personification ("the wind whispered to the trees"), synecdoche (referring to a whole thing by the name of one of its parts, such as calling a car "wheels," or calling a worker a "hand") and a number of other forms. When I speak to autism gatherings, I ask them to do two awareness things. First, to raise their hand if they catch me using figurative language, because I do it only a little less subconsciously than the average person, and the more

Much of our everyday conversation is imprecise and, to the child with autism, illogical.

I'm interrupted the more it illustrates my point. Then I send them off with a homework assignment—for twenty-four hours, record every example of figurative language they hear or catch themselves using. Try it yourself. You're going to be astonished.

So now you have an inkling of how much of our everyday conversation is imprecise and, to the child with autism, illogical. You'll learn even more quickly the first time you tell him to "wait just a minute for me" and he's not there when you come back in five.

And while we're on the subject of incomprehensible talk, expecting an autistic child to follow this kind of conversation is ludicrous: "We was talking and stuff, and I'm, like, I am SO not going there. And he just went, okay whatever, and I'm like FINE. Like I could care less, and then he goes, like, yeah bite me." Parents and teachers! It's more than okay to require siblings, classmates, and others to speak plainly around individuals with autism. Translated, the foregoing passage would sound like this: "I didn't want to talk with Jake anymore. We were both saying unkind things." Remember the scene in that irreverent old movie *Airplane*? "Pardon me, Stewardess, I speak jive." If different dialects, accents, and cadences of your own native language can be confusing to you, think of what a Tower of Babel they are to an autistic child.

To have a child who struggled with language was the ultimate irony for me. My college diploma reads Bachelor of Science, Speech Communication. The top shelf of our garage houses a crate of gently rusting high school debate trophies. Yes, I'm a certified windbag. I come from a family of inveterate punsters and wordmeisters, forever dreaming up obscure word games. I trod a major learning curve to, first, realize my child wasn't capable of or interested in this kind of verbal jousting, and second, accept that if I wanted to communicate meaningfully with him (and oh, how I did), I would have to rework my own manner of presentation. I had to think before I spoke. I had to carefully choose my words, my tone of voice, my inflection. If I didn't, he would tune me out, without malice, without annoyance, and without the slightest acknowledgment that I was even in the room.

And you thought this didn't happen until the teen years.

Editing your figurative language, getting into the practice of communicating with your child on his custom wavelength can be wearying, sometimes so much so that you may drift toward the kind of frustration spawning that unproductive mindset that this is somehow "special treatment" you shouldn't have to give. But remember that her having to decode your nonsense language is even more wearying and frustrating for her. Children with ASD can learn, in varying degrees, the various forms of figurative language.

I'm a concrete thinker. I interpret language literally.

When you use or hear an idiom or other figurative expression and rephrase it for her in concrete language, you teach that though it may seem strange, sometimes phrases may say one thing but mean something very different. Acknowledge that can seem silly, but also sometimes fun. Some kids like to keep a reference log of idioms they hear and learn. I know more than one youngster whose circumscribed interest is idioms.

While you work on framing your communication in more concrete terms, your child will give you gentle, judgment-free direction to keep you on track. When Bryce was quite young, his ultra-literal, concrete thought processes often confounded me. One day I discovered in the bathroom sink a Michael Jordan basketball action figure with a tub of Danish Orchards Raspberry Preserves dumped on top. This mystified me, no matter how I tried to interpret it. "What is this?" I finally asked Bryce. "Space Jam," he replied, having just seen the movie. I watched the crimson goo slithering down the drain. I couldn't think of a suitable response, nothing at all. So I did the sensible thing. I nodded and walked away. Later, it tickled our family to pieces when he learned to answer the telephone. My mother, a health professional with ample understanding of autism, nonetheless tripped herself up nearly every time she called. "Hi Bryce," she'd say. "What're you doing?" To which he would reply, "Well, Grandma, I'm talking to you on the phone." We all learned to ask more concrete questions, the kinds that lead to conversation. What did you do in science class today? What would you like to do on Saturday? What book are you reading this week? Even today, I catch myself babbling idioms to him and stop to check if he knows the one I just used. As an adult, he's learned (and uses) many idioms and other figurative phrases, and when he doesn't know a particular expression, he can identify it as figurative, given the context of the sentence.

51

But I'll never forget my most infamous slip-up, the one that seared into me how easily such mistakes, of all sizes, escape our well-intentioned lips and how adept our kids can sometimes be at letting us know.

Bryce was seven. We'd had an evening-long disagreement and inability to communicate that left both of us exhausted. I offered solution after solution, none of which he could believe or accept. (He "stood his ground.") We both grew frustrated, sweaty, and close to despair. With loving determination—and a small element of surprise—I was able to defuse the situation just before bedtime. We both earned our sweet dreams that night.

The next morning, we sat at our sunny breakfast table and I told him two things. First, that he could always trust me to be honest with him and act in his very best interest. Even if the solution to a problem seemed unpleasant, we'd still always find a way that worked for him. Then I told him I admired his tenacity, meaning that he maintained what he believed, didn't back down, resisted pressure. That took strength and courage. "You stuck to your guns," I said, "and that can be a good thing." The words hadn't cleared my lips before I knew I had goofed.

"I don't want to stick to a gun!" he declared, alarmed.

And then:

"Are you sure you didn't mean ... gum?"

Chapter Five

Listen to all the ways I'm trying to communicate.

It's hard for me to tell you what I need when I don't have a way to describe my thoughts and feelings. I may be hungry, frustrated, scared, or confused but right now I can't find those words. Be alert for body language, withdrawal, anxiety or other signs that something is wrong. They're there.

Or, when I can't find the words I need, I may recite words or whole scripts I've memorized from movies, videos, books or things other people say. Sometimes it makes me sound older than I am, and I may not completely understand all the words and meaning. I just know that it's a way I can answer when I'm expected to but can't in the "regular" way.

"You can't rush art."

Bryce turned his bottomless blue eyes on his first-grade teacher and delivered this zinger as she hustled the class to clean up their paints: "Quick-quick-quick! It's time for music! Brushes in the sink! Line up at the door! Let's go!" Bryce had just discovered the wonder of mixing orange and green paint to make brown for his version of Van Gogh's *Sunflowers*, and he didn't appreciate the hurry-scurry. His teacher couldn't wait to repeat his remark to me because "of course, he is right."

What she didn't know was that he lifted the response wholesale (words, inflection, and tempo), right out of *Toy Story 2*. Bryce had a breathtaking command of a verbal behavior called echolalia, repeating chunks of language he'd heard from others. When his own limited vocabulary failed him, he had split-second retrieval of functional responses from the encyclopedic stash of movie scripts stored on the hard drive of his brain.

Echolalia is common in autism. It can be immediate (child echoes something that has just been said to or near him), delayed (child repeats something he's heard in recent, mid- or distant past) or perseverative (child repeats the same phrase or question over and over again). For many parents (including me), echolalia incites a piercing sense of panic that foments when exchanges of fact, feeling, and thought cannot flow freely among ourselves, our child, and the rest of the world.

At the time of the can't-rush-art incident, ninety percent of Bryce's speech was delayed echolalia. He employed it so skillfully that it was largely undetectable to anyone but our family. Still, I was desperate to squash it—a common, understandable but misguided desire for parents in my position. Because the speech isn't spontaneous, it can seem like (since we're quoting movies) "what we've got here is failure to communicate." (*Cool Hand Luke*, 1967) Echolalic speech often doesn't seem to have any relevance to what's happening at the moment, although to the child, it does. He may be three or four associative links ahead of you, making it your tricky but necessary job to discover the correlation.

Echolalia is only one aspect of language development, albeit one that generates considerable emotion in parents. I have felt with a mother's heart, as you may be feeling, the urgency to have my child produce "normal" language, the kind that erases some of the stark difference between him and his same-age peers. In that urgency, we mustn't lose sight of the fact that while he has yet to develop basic vocabulary and the skills involved with generative speech, he still needs a way to communicate his needs, fears, and wants.

If you take away only one thing from this chapter, let it be this: having a means of functional communication, *whatever it may be*, is essential to any child, but more so to the child with autism. If your child can't get her needs met and fears quelled, her world and yours can be a horrid place. Without functional communication, expect to see her frustration and fear play out in behavior, as she tries to let you know by the only means available to her that things are not as they should be for her. Once she's comfortable that

> **Having a means of functional communication, *whatever it may be*, is essential to any child, but more so to the child with autism.**

she can communicate regardless of where she is between calm and calamity, and that you'll listen and hear her regardless of her mode of communication, she can begin to build an understanding of all facets of communication, including the ones that go beyond mere vocabulary.

The typical early words and petite first sentences of childhood seem so simple on the surface. You want your child to say "mama" and "doggie," then "I want juice" and "Can I play?" and "I love you." But oh, how much is going on in those simple phrases. Speech (the physical ability to produce vocal sounds) is only the beginning component of language (putting words together in a way that conveys meaning to others). Language alone doesn't create conversation (establishing social contact with others using verbal and nonverbal communication). As a baby, your child made his needs and moods known in nonverbal ways. Most children progress to uttering words, then stringing those words together into phrases and sentences. As they grow, their language becomes much more than a tool for labeling items, feelings, and actions. It becomes a means to express their thoughts and emotions, and to interact with others. The social use of language, called pragmatics, is the synergistic brew of words, gestures, facial expressions, and social understanding we use, often unconsciously or instinctively, to communicate with each other. At any one or many points along this developmental timeline, autism can hinder your child's development and understanding of these tools and how they work to connect us or separate us. In Chapter Eight, we'll further explore the social aspects of conversation, the everything-else beyond our words that helps us relate to others.

I can never forget how Bryce's early struggles with speech challenged his efforts to socialize, impacted his emotional health, and obscured his cognitive capabilities. Fortunately, two things happened concurrently that eased my mind enough that I could back off and let him work through his echolalia in his own way and at his own pace. First, I read an article by a twenty-year-old autistic man, successfully making his way through a four-year college. He described how he still employed echolalia in his everyday social communication, and that he alone knew it. I thought, *Huh. Maybe the stress I'm reaping on this issue isn't warranted.*

I called in our district autism specialist. She offered wise and memorable advice: "I know you want to stamp this out. But don't try to go around. Go through it. I promise you it won't last forever. Give him the time he needs to work through it." Encouraged by that advice, I was able to take a step back and see how my son and classmates like him used echolalia in a number of functional and interactive ways. They used it to:

- Reciprocate conversation, respond where he knows an exchange is expected.

- Ask for or request something, either an object or someone's attention.

- Offer information or opinion.

- Protest or deny the actions or requests of others.

- Give instructions or directives.

- Put a name or a label to an item, activity or place.

Though I didn't know the word for it at the time, Bryce was a gestalt learner. Gestalt is a German word that means whole or complete. Gestalt learners take experiences as one piece, without being able to see the individual components. Many autistic children learn language in this manner, absorbing it in chunks, rather than as individual words. As opposed to gestalt, we call word-by-word learning analytic. It may seem as though analytic language learners are more typical in the population than gestalt learners. In fact, many children with autism, particularly Asperger's, are analytic learners who can easily associate meaning with individual words. Both analytic and gestalt are legitimate ("normal") learning styles.

A speech therapist can guide your child through echolalia and other parts of language and communication development, including the process of learning to break apart "gestalts" and reconstruct the smaller pieces into spontaneous speech. Each child will have a unique response pattern. There's no correct timetable, and sometimes progress may look like regression. If your child spouts lengthy, eloquent scripts, his learning to generate simple sentences of his own may temporarily sound toddler-like. It's not. It's healthy language development. Remain mindful that producing words is one part of that development. Understanding what's being said, the context of it, the nuances, the often-baffling use of figurative language is the much larger task. Unfortunately, much of the communication that takes place in school settings assumes that all kids have a basic social brain that allows them to interpret all aspects of language. This is not true for kids with autism who, once past the hurdle of producing words, will continue to struggle with this if not given specific and sustained parent and professional guidance.

As a fourth-grader, Bryce sat for the usual round of triennial standardized testing, the results of which decreed his vocabulary to be severely subpar. This stunned me. Coming from three-word phrases at age four and ninety percent echolalic speech at age six, I marveled at his accomplishments with the spoken word by age ten, which included speaking with ease in front of groups. I asked to see the test material. Among other things, he had "incorrectly identified" the words cactus and violin. This brought my hackles up. Those words represented things that he seldom, if ever, encountered in his daily life, his reading, or his movie viewing. And he had gotten the context correct, identifying the cactus as a "desert plant" and the violin as a "music player." The rigidity of the testing infuriated me, but it did make me realize how, in listening to and responding to him, I automatically decoded the irregular language in both his spontaneous and echolalic speech. I didn't want to spend my conversational time with him correcting grammar and syntax, so I did the translation in my head and continued to exchange thoughts with him uninterrupted.

In one sense, I was doing the right thing, validating his means of functional communication and with it, his self-image. But I took the test results as a wake-up call that I needed to do more everyday feeding in of language as well as checking for comprehension in both the spoken and written word. For instance, we came across this passage in a story: "He ripped the handbag from her grasp." Bryce looked blank, so we stopped and I went over the words rip, grasp, and hand bag. "Oh," he said, exasperated. "He stole her purse. Why doesn't it just say that? 'He stole her purse?'" This led to a discussion of how words, like colors, come in many "shades" and how varying our words can make a story colorful. We had fun coming up with a long and comical list of ways to say big: large, huge, gigantic, immense, enormous, whopping, humongous, colossal, and on and on. It was a light bulb moment for both of us. He hadn't thought of words that way, and I hadn't thought of offering them so.

This reinforced one of the first and most elemental pieces of advice Bryce's speech therapist had given us: that we work hard to maintain a language-rich environment around him. A child not frequently exposed to other speaking people will develop language much more slowly. In particular, if your child is in a self-contained special education classroom, she may not have much exposure to typically developing kidspeak. Alongside using visual supports for our kids (we delve into that in Chapter Six), we must surround them with words and language. Among some of the countless ways to do this:

- Talk out the thoughts in your head, verbalize what you are doing and why.

- Acknowledge your child every time she speaks to you or otherwise attempts to communicate, regardless of whether you understand her.

- Read to her.

- Tell her stories.

- Sing to her. Singing is speech, so if your child learns songs easily, use that strength to enhance her language skills. Talk about any new words in the song she may not understand.

- When reading or singing, distinguish nonsense words from real words.

Putting your child on the spot to respond in words or engage in conversation can be very stressful, so help ease that performance anxiety by putting manageable parameters on verbal exchanges. Try this two-minute/two-minute rule: tell him you'd like to hear about his day at school, his favorite toy or book, the dog, or any subject that interests him. If he's willing, give him two minutes to gather his thoughts, then watch, listen and respond to him for two minutes. In family conversation, learn to pause for responses. Many families chat and banter at a rapid-fire pace that leaves the child with autism unable to keep up. To slow the overall pace of exchanges and give your child a better chance to participate, wait a few seconds before responding.

"Use your words." As you push your child or student toward verbal communication, how many times have you prompted him to do this, and with how many different inflections? One day encouraging, gently coaxing. The next day stern, with a shot of frustration. Another day, weary and pleading. All the words your child has may not be enough to make his needs, wants, thoughts, and ideas known. She may have learned a word, but producing it requires added layers of processing and skill. Articulating her thoughts and feelings may be easy one day, impossible the next when sensory issues amplify and interfere, or when your expectation that she maintain certain behaviors depletes all the energy she can muster. Think you know how it feels to be forced to multi-task under pressure? Your child or student's list includes trying to self-regulate multiple hyper- or hypoactive senses simultaneously, intercept and interpret visual and auditory clues and cues floating around, use social observation and interpretation to problem solve what to say and do, and then produce language as well. "Use your words" is a worthy goal, as so many cultures consider speech to be the ultimate portable, standalone, all-terrain, all-hours, all-weather communication device. But on the way to achieving any degree of that goal, it's compulsory that we acknowledge and facilitate all our child's or student's attempts to communicate, in whatever form the message comes.

Acknowledge and accept that those attempts that don't include words, that come from behavior or silence, are rich in communication. None of us get through life without our moments of "being at a loss for words." So even when a child has words to use, honor her behavior as an attempt to communicate in the only way she may be able to at that moment. Likewise, a child's silence can be eloquent communication. Consider the directive, "Answer me!", so often uttered in frustration, exasperation, or anger when a child's response doesn't come in the words and manner we expect. When silence is the response, consider the many possible perspectives the child may harbor but can't articulate:

- I didn't understand you. Try a different way.

- Your words hurt me.

- You made me angry.

- I don't have a response.

- You misjudged me.

- You taught me to ignore people who speak to me disrespect-fully.

61

Getting into the practice of communicating with your child on his custom wavelength is excellent preparation for those teen years, when your child will treat you to typical teen behaviors alongside her autism-influenced ones. Starting now, listen to everything your child wants to tell you, in whatever form it comes. Look at him when he speaks or otherwise attempts to communicate with you, and answer him every time, in a manner that is meaningful to him. Setting up that reciprocal exchange (he hears you, you hear him) gives him confidence in the value of his message, whatever it may be and however it may be delivered. That confidence will become the motivation that moves him beyond concrete responses to spontaneous offerings, and on to initiating thoughtful and thought-filled conversation, something parents and teachers of language-challenged children alike yearn for.

And after investing so much heartfelt effort in helping our children find their words, you may find that a great irony of the twenty-first century sneaks in to ambush you. Without ongoing attention, that language-rich environment can slip away, disappearing into the crevices of technology and changing culture. Even when our kids do achieve the ability to speak, reciprocal speech, of any duration, may be a hard-won learned skill. The essential component of any learned skill is practice, practice, and more practice. And that's why a sad realization came to me during an ordinary morning round of errands, one poignant and worrisome reason why reciprocal speech remains a challenge for our kids: we no longer talk to the people in our immediate community. My morning was a potent example. I got cash from an ATM; I didn't talk to a bank teller. I scanned my groceries through the self-checkout line; I didn't talk to a checker. Our library has automated checkout; I didn't talk to the librarian. I mailed a package at the Automated Postal Center without talking to a clerk. I'd bypassed at least half a dozen of what, not so long ago,

Listen to all the ways I'm trying to communicate.

would have been opportunities for human interaction. Former *Wall Street Journal* publisher Les Hinton has been quoted as saying that the scarcest resource of the twenty-first century, "after water and food and all of that," will be human attention.

A language-rich environment? More like a language-depleted landscape.

Automation, electronic communication and social media have a legitimate, immutable place in our culture. But if we value the stimulation, joy, and functionality of reciprocal speech—conversation—we must teach our children, by example, to come out from behind their computer and tablet and phone screens and practice talking to others. Our speech therapist's advice about creating a language-rich environment came at a time when the use of language hadn't yet been appropriated by electronics, when being conversational included vocal inflections, facial expression, and body language. You know, like Skype without the screen. Of the many parent-teen conflicts my husband and I expected to face, we never dreamed we'd be considered counter-culture because we wanted our children to speak to other humans.

Sooner or later, our kids will have to talk to the people in their community because some relationships cannot be relegated to a screen—the doctor, the dentist, the bus driver, the hair stylist, the flight attendant, the policeman, the firefighter, the clergy, the lifeguard, the piano teacher, the coach, the lawyer, the judge. It will happen if we help our children expand their communication skills by respecting their current abilities, and providing a variety of means to convey wants, needs, thoughts, feelings, and ideas under all circumstances. We've then opened a door to a place where they can experience conversation as camaraderie rather than combat, to a place where genuine communication connects us all.

Chapter Six

Picture this! I'm visually oriented.

Show me how to do something rather than just telling me. I may need you to show me many times and in more than one way.

Picture and word charts, schedules, reminders and other visual instructions help me move through my day. They keep me from stressing over having to remember what comes next. When I can look at something, it helps me remember what to do and when to do it, and that helps me stay organized in my brain, which helps me stay calm. Then I can move smoothly from one activity to the next, and be better at doing what you expect of me.

I need to see something to learn it, because the things you say to me are like steam. The words evaporate in an instant, before I have a chance to make sense of them. Instructions and information presented to me visually can stay in front of me for as long as I need, and will be just the same when I come back to them later.

One of my favorite spunky girls is *My Fair Lady*'s Eliza Doolittle, a character created as a walking, breathing language experiment. She makes herself impossible to ignore in a number of ways, never more so than in the song "Show Me," when she admonishes her lover to knock it off with the "Words, words, words! I'm so sick of words!" followed by, "Don't waste my time, show me!"

Many autistic children would cheer her sentiments.

Visual cueing is hardly a novelty or "special accommodation." If you use any kind of calendar or planner device (electronic or paper) or keep a to-do list on your desk or wall, you're using a visual support. The apps, maps, menus, mirrors, videos, cameras and watches you likely use every day are all visual supports. Sign language—I've seen it called handspeak—is a highly developed form of visual communication that includes facial expression and body language in a manner similar to how vocal volume and inflection enhance the meaning of spoken language. Semaphore uses flag signals rather than words and letters to communicate visually across distances. Go to a baseball game and watch the third base coach rub his forearm, grab his belt and slap his chest. He's not auditioning for a Jane Goodall film. He's telling his base runner to stay put unless the ball is a hopper to shallow right field. All these modes of interface use something other than spoken words to achieve functional communication.

> The ability to communicate, to receive, express and feel heard, is fundamental to the overall healthy functioning of your child, of any person.

Your child or student may have a profound need for visual cueing. Many individuals with autism think in images, not words. Their primary language is pictorial, not verbal. A child may have minimal spoken expressive language, but are we arrogant enough, or naïve enough, to think this means he has no thoughts, preferences, opinions, ideas, or beliefs, that he has nothing to say? Does that tree falling in the woods make no sound because no one is around to hear it? Nonsense. Your child or student may be translating his life experiences into pictures in his head. If so, it's a language no less legitimate than the one you use, and it's the one you must accommodate if you want to reach and teach him in a meaningful way that leads to meaningful results.

Dr. Temple Grandin elevated the world's awareness of her visual orientation in her 1996 book *Thinking in Pictures*, which opens:

"I think in pictures. Words are like a second language to me. I translate both spoken and written words into full-color movies, complete with sound, which run like a VCR tape in my head. When somebody speaks to me, his words are instantly translated into pictures. Language-based thinkers often find this phenomenon difficult to understand."

As we established in Chapter Five, the ability to communicate, to receive, express and feel heard, is fundamental to the overall healthy functioning of your child, of any person. Without an effective means of communication, a visually-oriented child (square peg) continually being squeezed into a speech-oriented world (round hole) is bound to feel unheard, embattled, overwhelmed, and outnumbered. What should she do, but retreat?

Creating a visual schedule or other visual strategy to help your child navigate his school day or home routine may be one of the first tools suggested by your school team or by your own research. Why? Because it:

- Provides the structure and predictability essential to autistic children. Knowing what happens next frees her to focus on the task or activity at hand without the anxiety of worrying about what comes next and when.

- Serves as a touchstone, a consistent source of information that enables her to trust that events will unfold logically and she can feel safe in that routine.

- Reinforces the first/then strategy for dealing with less enjoyable tasks. "First you finish eight math problems, then you may have five minutes of choice time" helps him feel motivated rather than lapsing into avoidance or procrastination.

- Increases his ability to perform tasks autonomously and to transition between activities independently.

- Can help ease the rigidity of thinking and inflexibility that frequently characterize autism. As the child's confidence in his independence grows, you can insert curveballs into the schedule in the form of varied activities, or a question mark, indicating a surprise activity.

- Can incorporate social skill-building. The schedule might include a five-minute "play [or read] with a classmate" time or "say or wave goodbye to three people."

All of this builds and fortifies your child or student's ability to understand and work toward meeting the expectations of those around him (assuming those expectations are reasonable and achievable given his current stage of development).

Not all visual schedules are created equal any more than all calendars are. The common element is their sequential nature. Beyond that, the size, style of representation, portability, and length vary infinitely.

We employed Bryce's first visual schedule when he entered Pre-K, long before the convenience and flexibility of handheld electronic devices and apps. We used a system of simple line drawings to depict the sequential activities of the day's routine: get up, eat breakfast, get dressed, brush teeth, get on bus. After introducing him to the schedule, teaching how to use it, and walking through it with him for a few days, Bryce did each task independently, but he never seemed engaged in the picture system or showed any interest in expanding upon it. A year later, we discovered that Bryce didn't relate to artwork. Stick figures had little meaning for him, nor did he want anything to do with fanciful or abstract illustration. He liked concrete images—photographs. He engaged with enthusiasm when I presented stories or instructions with photographs.

Whether electronic, paper, or other medium, the first step in creating a successful visual communication strategy is to identify your child or student's level of representation. That's fancy talk for determining what type of visual is meaningful to him. Bryce required photographs; for another child, it might be stick figures, pencil drawings or full-color art. More concrete-thinking children may need to begin at the very basic level of the physical object. As the child grows older and her communication skills expand, it might be words in combination with pictures, and perhaps someday, words alone (then it gets called a to-do list). This attention to modification as the child ages and learns is a key element of the effectiveness of visual supports, ensuring that they continue to be useful in a manner that doesn't invite ridicule or ostracism. Consider as well how your child best tracks information. Don't assume it's left to right. It may be top to bottom. An occupational therapist can help you determine this. How many increments should appear on a schedule or a page at one time? Don't overwhelm. Start with two or three and work up from there.

Visual strategies aren't something to phase out as your child becomes progressively more independent. They're life-long tools that foster organization, time management, flexibility, initiative, and a host of other executive functioning skills necessary for self-sufficiency. Over time, I keep coming up against gentle reminders that a visual schedule is more than a strip of stick-figure sketches that we used to help Bryce learn to get ready for preschool. The level of representation and sophistication may escalate with the years, but not the need, and not the stability it provides and the stress it relieves. It's what keeps the calendar printers and app designers in business. Occasionally I hear from someone who says visual supports for kids with autism are a "crutch," which, forgive me, usually sounds like shorthand for "I don't want to go to the effort to provide that." I posted a meme about this, and an autistic adult shot back with, "Crutches are invaluable tools that help people maintain mobility when they otherwise wouldn't be able to get around."

In the first weeks of middle school, in a new building full of new teachers and a sea of new faces, Bryce faced a formidable challenge. Outdoor School was a popular program in our county wherein sixth graders went to local camps for a week to learn about native ecosystems. It was a terrific program, but one that raised many questions on both my part and Bryce's. He'd never spent five nights away from home without family. He would be under the supervision of two teachers who had known him less than six weeks, and the rest of the camp staff, who didn't know him at all. He would have to tolerate unfamiliar routine, unpredictable weather, sleeping and eating with children he had never met before, and perhaps worst of all—camp food.

Although both school and camp staff assured me they would make any accommodation necessary, Bryce wasn't sure he wanted to go, changing his mind from hour to hour. We drove to the camp for visitation, through which he remained silent. He surveyed the dining room, which would be, he was sure, a source of misery. But wait—a spark of interest! On the wall by the door, larger than life, hung the daily schedule: 6:45 wake up, 7:15 flag, 7:30 breakfast, 10:30 wildlife studies, 11:15 lunch, etc. on through 6:30 campfire. The whole day, mapped out in manageable increments.

"Would somebody get me a copy of this?" he asked.

The staff happily made him a palm-size schedule strung on a lanyard. The head cook gave us a meal-by-meal schedule, so he would know when he would eat camp food and when he would ask for one of his own meals I sent with him.

Bryce's teacher reported that, armed with his two frequently consulted visual schedules, he had easily settled in. The visual schedules gave him predictability and a concrete routine that made the exotic, intimidating setting not only manageable but enjoyable. Bryce organized and directed his cabin's skit, a spoof on the morning inspection routine. At the final campfire, he moved his teacher to tears as he spoke about feeling unsure when he arrived but making new friends throughout the week. He wore the same pair of socks the entire week and ignored the other five pairs in his bag. He had a typical Outdoor School experience and he spent the rest of the year telling anyone who asked that it was the best part of sixth grade.

For teaching to be effective, you must be heard, and many children with autism hear better with a visual. Also recognize that what happens between the words and the picture is translation and teaching. Just because a child is a visually-oriented learner doesn't mean he'll automatically know to use a visual support if all you do is show it to him. You'll need to teach about the how, when, and why of using it. You may need to slow down your usual pace of spoken communication to allow that processing to happen. Give her extra time to respond, don't repeat the same instructions over and over if they're not getting through. "Please don't 'expline!'" Eliza Doolittle scolds. "Show me!"

The success your child achieves with the aid of his visual supports may leave you sighing in relief and satisfaction, thinking "I don't know what we'd do without them." That's your cue to take steps to ensure you never have to find out. You need backup or contingency plans and tools, because electronic devices glitch, mysteriously lose files, run out of power at the worst possible moments, get lost or stolen, go through the laundry, fall into the bathtub or toilet. Nonelectronic supports are no less subject to physical damage or loss. Having a Plan B at the ready when the child's primary support fails is as important as having the supports in the first place. I'm cautious myself in this regard, keeping both electronic and paper calendars, knowing there will be at least several times a year when, for purposes of portability (tablets or other electronics in the pouring rain at Outdoor School wouldn't have been an option), cross-reference, or where-the-heck-did-I-leave-that-dang-phone, I'll be glad I did.

For many autistic children, visuals make sense where oral or written words don't. Picture it (get it?) this way: visual images are the powerful medium that organizes and explains your child's world, tames its stress, gives him understandable guidance and boundaries. See it his way; teach him in a way that makes sense to him. Life then becomes less of a battle and he need be less of a warrior. He comes, he sees—he conquers.

Chapter Seven

Focus and build on what I can do
rather than what I can't do.

I can't learn if I'm always made to feel that I'm not good enough and that I need to be fixed. I don't want to try anything new when I'm sure all I'll hear is how I got it wrong, no matter how nicely you think you're saying it. I *am* trying harder.

Look for my strengths and you'll find them. There's more than one right way to do most things.

When my brother first read *Ten Things* he commented, "Number seven is true for all kids." He's right, and I would extend it to all people, not just kids, not just those with autism.

Yet many families and educators unwittingly tumble into the Swamp of Unmet Expectations. This is where a child's potential goes to die if we as adults fail to detach our personal aspirations from those appropriate for our child.

Adapted PE teacher Sarah Spella sees it all the time. "Parents get into a grieving process," she says. "Their child isn't going to be a certain way that they expected her to be, and their attitude becomes a huge handicap for the child. I see many cases where the parent may be very much into physical fitness and sports. Their too-high expectations in that area can turn the child completely off to the very things the parent wants him to be. I work with these children every week, and they don't care a hoot for PE." They may have skills on par with their typically developing peers, she explains, but they process those skills differently, and it all means nothing without a belief system behind it. "I can tell them for years, I know you can do this. But if they don't have that full parental support, there is only so much I can do in thirty minutes a week."

Each of us is a unique blend of ability and disability. As George Carlin put it, "Barry Bonds can't play the cello and Yo-Yo Ma can't hit the curveball." My husband can't write books and I can't engineer industrial air-flow systems. It never comes up for discussion; we're happy knowing that our different skills and abilities mean we each have a constructive place in the world.

I've read my share of sad emails and stories that echo the can't-do lament of parents, but nevertheless have potential for happy endings. "Four generations of Andersons have played the violin, and I can't even get him to look at one." No kidding. Is there a musical instrument more sensory-hellish than a violin? Imagine the screechy sound a new learner produces, the strings that bite into tender fingers and the sensation of having a weirdly shaped vibrating box parked under your sweaty chin while you hold both arms at unnatural angles. It took someone outside this family to notice that the child, while not inclined to the violin, was a natural at golf, with an easy and accurate swing. I hope the family took the opportunity not only to learn something new from their child but also to validate his capability.

Another family, passionate skiers, gloomily accepted that their child's vestibular issues made skiing and snowboarding abhorrent to him. While at the beach one summer, Mom noticed her son could spend hours moving piles of sand around, examining them from every angle, making structural adjustments. That winter she bought him a set of snow block molds (plain plastic boxes)

Being able to focus and build on the can-do rather than can't-do of your child is all about perspective.

and away he went building igloos, forts, and castles. Her discovery of what he could do rather than what he couldn't do meant that the family could still spend a day together on the mountain, with each family member rotating "Andy time" with the snow forts while the others skied. Eventually, Andy acclimated to the snow enough to try gentle inner-tubing and snowshoeing.

Being able to focus and build on the can-do rather than can't-do of your child is all about perspective. Earlier in the book we talked about reframing your child's challenging behaviors as positives. It bears repeating. Is the child standoffish, or able to work independently? Is he reckless, or adventuresome and willing to try new experiences? Is he compulsively neat, or does he have outstanding organizational skills? Do you hear nonstop pestering with questions, or do you hear curiosity, tenacity, and persistence? Later in the chapter, we'll talk more about how the perspective you hold about your child and his abilities now will directly affect his ability to grow into self-sufficient adulthood. For now, I ask:

Can you do this? Can you shift perspective, build upon all that is positive in your child?

Will you do this?

My father marveled that he had "never, ever known a happier baby" than Bryce, adding, "and I've been around a lot of babies." I agreed. Bryce, a sweet and placid infant, went everywhere with me.

We enrolled him in a preschool program two mornings a week when he was two. September wasn't yet over before the teacher reported that Bryce played in a corner by himself, his language skills were underdeveloped, he didn't participate in table activities and he hit and pushed his classmates. I struggled to believe this because it was so out of character. By spring conference time, nothing had changed. "Bryce usually plays by himself," repeated the written report. "He's quiet and will observe other children. He has a hard time following directions. Bryce doesn't like art projects or table activities. He says words but we have a hard time understanding him. He imitates the other children. Bryce has a short attention span. He doesn't interact during circle time."

Wow, I thought. *That's a damn lot of can'ts. He's* two.

The recitation of can't/doesn't carried into the next year. At November parent conferences, I politely interrupted the teacher to ask if we could refocus on things that Bryce could and did do. With this prompt, I heard how he entertained himself for long periods, loved physical play whether indoors or out, sought out sand table

Focus and build on what I can do rather than what I can't do.

---

play, and had a gift for imitation. We concluded that his language delays interfered substantially with his ability to become part of the classroom community. I thought, here is something I could do, and we entered the world of speech therapy. Soon, he was putting together intelligible three-word phrases at school.

Still, my asking for focus on can-do and enlisting professional help didn't improve the big picture. The winter report came, by now wearyingly familiar: wants to interact with other children but doesn't know how, plays by himself, has a hard time listening in a group situation. I felt the time had come to stop the spinning. I asked for a meeting with the teachers and the school principal. After listening yet again to the same can'ts, a touchy exchange unfolded in which I asked the teacher flat out if maybe she didn't like Bryce. She reacted as if she'd been shot. I instantly felt crummy-and-a-half, wondering if I had poisoned the productivity out of the meeting. "No, it's a legitimate question," said the principal. "You had to ask." The answer was that Bryce's teachers loved him, but his needs were beyond their ability to handle within the resources of the school. The meeting ended with the principal's decision to refer him to public Early Intervention services.

"What is that?" I asked, having never heard the term "early intervention." What was happening?

"They are people who will help," she said. And the Early Intervention teachers and therapists were remarkable can-do people. They continually told me how "cool" Bryce was (and why), how far they thought he could go, and how we could chart the journey to get there. They focused on his strengths and on teaching tactics and physical accommodations to ameliorate his challenges. It resonated with us all, Bryce included.

The earliest books I read on the subject of autism told a different story, one fraught with dismal assumptions. He wouldn't be able to form relationships, wouldn't get married, wouldn't be able to hold a job, wouldn't understand the nuances of the law or the banking system or the bus system. Splayed on the page in black and white, more nay-saying, written by people who supposedly knew more than I did. I am not, I told myself, in denial. And already, deep in the space between the gray matter and the heart, a tiny voice strained to be heard. *Don't believe it. It isn't true unless you let it be.* I had just started out but I was already done listening to the nay-sayers and their choruses of can't. I had everything to gain and nothing to lose by heeding the first advice our pediatrician ever gave me: "Trust your instinct. You know more than you think you know." With the exception of marriage, Bryce did all those wouldn'ts before the age of twenty.

> **One of the most important things you can do as a parent is to heed the strong inner voice that tells you what is right for your child.**

One of the most important things you can do as a parent is to heed the strong inner voice that tells you what is right for your child. This shift in perspective from can't to won't needs to come from your heart as well as your brain. It calls you to give equal consideration to what you feel or intuit as to what you "know" or "think," that you weigh "evidence-based" and "best practices" against the bundle of evidence that is the child in your arms and before your eyes every day. No one else loves her as you do and no one else is as invested in her future. The most popular treatments and thinking of the day may be right for many children but may not be for yours. One particular approach to autism was prevalent in the early 1990s. I read about it, loathed it, knew with 200% certainty that it wouldn't work with Bryce, and during a memorable school meeting, told those can-do early intervention people: "Do this to my kid and I will kill you." Happily for me, they had already decided the same thing (the teacher later told me she wanted to stand and applaud). Most of them are still in my life, now cherished friends, and boy, do they remember that conversation.

I realize you may find the preceding paragraph provocative. Since writing the first edition of this book I'm asked regularly, sometimes nastily, to reveal the approach I so loathed. My answer is always the same. I'm not going to tell you what it was, because if you ask the question, you missed the point. The take-away of my story is that you educate yourself about resources available and pursue only those that make sense for your child.

My can-do attitude about Bryce grew strong in the face of my early confrontations with can't-do. That's not to say the can't-do messages I received about him didn't scare me; of course they scared me. They also challenged me, made me mad, made me think: *Oh yeah? We'll see about that.*

If you haven't been in the habit of conscientiously focusing on what your child can do, how do you start? First, acknowledge that this is a shift in mindset, and it will take time and practice. Next, look for an indication of your child's learning style.

"Do not ask how smart is my child, but how is my child smart?" counsels David Sousa, author of *How the Brain Learns*. Typically developing children may learn in a variety of ways. Children with autism may favor one learning style almost to exclusion of others. Here's what that might look like:

Sequential learners benefit from step-by-step instructions, frequently excel at rote memorization, may be called neat freaks (a subtly derogatory phrase that needs to go) because they like visual organization.

Gestalt or global learners assimilate information in chunks, sizing up the big picture first, then chunking it down into details.

Naturalist learners learn best in natural settings. They like to interact with animals and the outdoors, and may demonstrate an unusual ability to sort, categorize, organize, or preserve information.

Kinesthetic learners learn by doing, seeking to experience the world through movement. They are climbers, runners, dancers, actors; they enjoy crafts and tools.

Spatial learners are your little construction workers or chess players. He likes to plan and/or build and draw things he sees in his head, and he relates well to maps, puzzles, charts, and graphs. He seems to have an inborn understanding of concepts of physics and geometry, but may be poor at spelling and memorizing verbal passages.

Musical learners perceive patterns in sound (rhythms, rhymes, raps), hold melodies in their heads, and compose their own tunes as mnemonic devices. Many autistic children who are hypersensitive to noise and have delayed verbal skills may be musical learners.

Understanding how your child or student processes information opens the floodgates to learning. You'll be able to guide her to success in activities inside and outside school through which she can experience the self-confidence necessary to confront tasks or events that challenge her. You'll be more flexible and enthusiastic in your approach, and you'll see it in the increased enthusiasm she will have for learning because finally, it makes some sense to her.

In doing so, you must throw out conventional or typical growth charts and timelines you may see in books or doctors' offices. Much of it is irrelevant to your child. At the outset of my journey, I learned that one of the hallmarks of autism is uneven development. One of Bryce's early friends was a four-year-old oceanography wiz who had forgotten more about coral reef habitats and bioluminescence than I will ever know. His mother told me she would trade it all for a few moments of social connection and a smile like Bryce's. A devoted advocate and learner herself, she eventually got both.

Bryce does have a brilliant smile, but the conventional timelines have been meaningless for him in many ways. He didn't talk reliably until age four, and didn't read reliably until the fourth grade. He loved swimming pools but clung to the sides, a blond barnacle, steadfastly refusing swim lessons until age eight when, with the right teacher and the right pool, he churned through all six levels of the swim program in just a few months. His instructors told us that most kids get stuck at a certain level, sometimes for months, before moving on. As he did with his language development, Bryce learned to swim in a gestalt manner—big, albeit delayed, chunks rather than the more typical progression of little steps.

And now a word about our responsibilities and vulnerabilities as parents, family members, and teachers in can-do vs. can't-do. One of the most distressing Internet posts I ever read popped up on a site whose members were having a spirited discussion about my *Ten Things*. One mom, who admitted to feeling "tired and snarky," ended a long I-love-you-but message to her child with this: "Oh, and God, if you're listening, I take back what I stupidly vowed when she was small and adorable and didn't hit me, about not wanting her any other way than what she was. I'll take that trade-in now, for the kid she was supposed to be."

I wanted to both weep and rage when I read this because I'm beyond certain her child hasn't asked God if she can trade in her mother for the parent she was supposed to be. I weep for the everyday magic this mom will miss in her child, the opportunities and accomplishments drowned in the stew of bitterness. I rage at the no-win situation in which she's placed her child, the unfairness of blaming autism for even the regular-kid things she does: "Don't feed almonds and Barbie parts to the dog. I don't appreciate the extra mess."

Though I empathized with this mother's soul-crushing fatigue, and though most of her post was snarly, I could still pick out building blocks of hope that had the power to turn the whole thing around. She worried for the future of her child as an adult and she wanted to lessen the impact of her child's autism on the siblings. She engaged her child in occupational and speech therapies (albeit referred to as "tortures"); she weighed the pros and cons of medications. So while her harsh words made me cringe, I can hope she found her way to building on what both she and her child can do.

"Whether you think you can or whether you think you can't, you're probably right." That's Henry Ford, icon of American industrialism, and a person who some think occupied a spot on the autism spectrum. An authentic diagnosis is lost to history, but the diagnosis is less important than the message: what you choose to believe about your child's autism might be the single biggest factor in his outcome as an adult.

What we choose to believe isn't always verifiable truth, and how deeply we believe it isn't the test of its veracity. I may believe with all my heart that I can fly under my own power, and stuff a grand piano up my nose, but that won't make it true. The larger significance lies in what we choose to believe where no tangible evidence exists, and how we will allow that choosing to direct our actions.

If you're treading quicksand in the swamp of what-might-have-been, you can be sure that's the message your child gets. You're a rare

Focus and build on what I can do rather than what I can't do.

---

person if being constantly reminded of your shortcomings spurs you to improve. For the rest of us, it's a self-esteem squasher. Time to grab for that overhead vine and realize that only a pencil dot separates "bitter" and "better."

When a diagnosis of autism comes in, many parents feel overwhelming urgency. They rush to read everything about autism they can get their hands on, join online discussion groups and network like mad with other parents. Sometimes the ensuing crush of information overwhelms. Some of it is encouraging and uplifting; some of it is depressing and spirit-sapping. There are professionals to consult, school and therapy programs to put into action, medications and special diets to consider, and worries about how to pay for it. If you allow this avalanche of new information to overtake you, you risk overdosing on the very tools that are going to get you through the long haul ahead. Paralysis sets in. It's real; it happens.

Here is one thing you can do. Adjust yourself to this new challenge at a measured, reasonable pace by knowing this:

You have time. You have lots of time.

You have today.

You have tomorrow.

You have next week.

You have next month and next year, and many years after that.

Every passing year brings new information and understanding, for you, and for the fields of medicine and education.

Tune out the naysayers. Stay the course. Results will come.

Chapter Eight

Help me be social.

You make it look easy, but being "social" is very hard for me. What's obvious about it to you isn't obvious to me—it's baffling and confusing. It may look like I don't want to play with other kids on the playground, but that may be because I don't know how to join in or I can't follow how fast their ideas change minute to minute. If I laugh when Emily falls off the slide, it's not that I think it's funny. It's that I don't know what to say. In school, working in a group may feel uncomfortable, since I do better when I work by myself.

Don't assume that because I may be smart I understand what it means to be social. I can't learn it just by watching others.

We can be blunt with each other here. Kids at almost any point on the spectrum often stand out as socially offbeat. The heartbreak it causes, to the child and to the parent, stirs in many parents an intense need to fix that facet of their child. If social competence was a physiological function, we could throw medication, nutrition, exercise, or physical therapy at it and make it happen. If kids with autism were curious, outgoing, motivated learners, we could cultivate social intelligence curriculum-style.

Too often, our kids aren't like that, and social awareness isn't a set of concrete, itemized skills. Basic manners (please and thank you, wipe nose on tissue not sleeve, wait your turn) can and must be taught, regardless of the child's level of function, but learning to be at ease among others in the bustle and nuances of daily life is infinitely more complex. Think about all the different physical venues and social environments of your daily life. Each has a web of social behaviors within which we judge each other, and each has its own social rules that are generally known in varying degree but rarely taught.

Despite what you may read or hear from sources and contacts both professional and personal, social skills (behaviors we want our child to exhibit) aren't the end product of what we need to teach our children. The ultimate goal of helping our children learn to navigate the ever-shifting social world is for them to become socially competent—able to walk into any social situation and figure out what to say, what to do, and how to manage it internally and externally. Focusing on social competence rather than teaching social skills is a perspective now recognized in educational and therapeutic circles and espoused for its emphasis on social-emotional intelligence as a determining factor in a child's success in life. As Bryce's high school principal stressed to his students over and over, "Lack of social competence will get you fired from a job faster than lack of cognitive skills or intelligence."

Breaking down the synergistic world of social-emotional intelligence isn't easy or natural for many adults, given that most of us were left to learn it intuitively. Today we have success-oriented books and blogs with topics like "learning to work in a group" or "four steps to joining a conversation," and this is exactly the type of teaching most autistic kids need. Just as we all had to learn to walk before we could run, we must teach our children to "think social" before they can act social, and do that with understanding and positive intent, not just by rote repetition or in fear of consequences. To be a strong social thinker your child will face the challenge of factoring context and perspective into his actions—to consider the physical, social, and temporal aspects of his surroundings, to take into account the thoughts and feelings of others, to use shared imagination to connect with a play partner, and to comprehend that others have favorable or not-so-favorable thoughts and reactions to him based on what he says and does in a particular situation. Social-emotional intelligence is the source from which our social behaviors and social competence springs, and it may be a bigger determinant in a child's long-term success in life than cognitive intelligence.

We must teach our children to "think social" before they can act social.

Parent or teacher, home or school, teaching a child with autism to be a social thinker, to observe and navigate a social situation, begins with chucking any assumptions you may harbor about his ability to absorb social sensibility by simply being around and observing socially adept people, or that he will somehow, someday outgrow his social cluelessness. Some of today's education systems and the various standards that guide their operations, do incorporate socially-based concepts into their curriculum standards.

Unfortunately, at this writing some still operate on the flawed supposition that all children enter the world with an intact social processing brain operating on a presumed social developmental progression. It makes no sense (and is grossly unfair to the child) to respond to a child's social snafus based on such assumptions and then blame his autism when our attempts to teach

Social-emotional intelligence may be a bigger determinant in a child's long-term success in life than cognitive intelligence.

don't register with him. What our children need is for us to shift perspective and start building their social awareness at its roots.

When we say we want our child to learn social skills, we're really reaching for something grander. We want him to be able to fit into the world around him, to function independently at school, in the community, at work, and within his personal relationships. Bryce stated this goal from early adolescence and, he told me, it had always been his goal, long before he could articulate it or even put a name to it in his childhood thoughts. More than playing by a rule book, being social is a state of confident being that grows with careful nurturing of social awareness and social connection skills, starting when a child is very young:

- Joint experience: being able to make basic connections with other people and learning that others are vast and beneficial information sources.

- Perspective taking: being able to see and experience the world from standpoints other than your own, and to see these different perspectives as opportunities to learn and grow.

- Flexibility: being able to roll with unforeseen changes in routine and expectation, being able to recognize that mistakes aren't an end result but a part of learning and growing, and that disappointments are matters of degree.

- Curiosity: drawing motivation from thinking about the "why" behind things—why something exists, why its existence is important, why others feel the way they do, and how it reflects back and matters to us.

- Self-esteem: believing enough in your own abilities to risk trying new things, having enough respect and affection for yourself to be able to deflect the cruel and thoughtless remarks and actions of others as saying more about them than you.

- Big picture thinking: appreciating that we use our social brains and our social know-how whether or not we are interacting with others. We read stories, trying to figure out the motives of characters and predict what they will do next. We replay situations in our head, deciding whether or not we acted appropriately. Your child may tell you, "I don't care about being social; I'm happy by myself." He may mean it in the moment, and many people do generally prefer solitude to socializing. But it's also true that some of our kids adopt the I-don't-care attitude to deflect the pain of caring very much and not having the knowledge, skills, and support to overcome their social barriers, and in doing so, achieve their goals and dreams in life.

- Communication: understanding that we communicate even when we are not talking.

Michelle Garcia Winner coined the term "Social Thinking" in the mid 1990s, and is one of the leading voices in the field of social-emotional learning. In one of her many books on Social Thinking®, she outlines the Four Steps of Communication that unfold in linear sequence, within milliseconds, and often without conscious thought:

- We think about other people's thoughts and feelings as well as our own

- We establish physical presence so people understand our intention to communicate

- We use our eyes to monitor how people are feeling, acting, and reacting to what is happening between us

- We use language to relate to others

Did you notice that language enters the communication equation only as the last step? And yet it's where, as parents and teachers, we typically place emphasis. Teaching only step four in the absence of the other three results in your child or student being inadequately equipped, vulnerable, and likely to be less effective, less successful in her social communication. Winner calls this emphasis on teaching at the level of behavior "teaching in the leaves" when what our autistic kids need is social education that starts at the roots.

It's equally important to imbue your child with a sense of the role nonverbal communication plays in his social encounters. The junctures at which the subtleties of social interaction can go awry fall into three broad categories:

- Vocalic communication: He doesn't understand the myriad nuances of spoken language. He doesn't understand sarcasm, puns, idioms, metaphors, hints, slang, double entendres, hyperbole, or abstraction. He may speak in a monotone (suggesting boredom to the listener), or he may speak too loudly, too softly, too quickly, or too slowly.

- Kinesthetic communication: He doesn't understand body

language, facial expressions, or emotional responses (crying, recoiling). He may use gestures or postures inappropriately and may refuse eye contact. So many of our kids lack even the basic understanding that our eyes are information sources. Dr. Temple Grandin related that she didn't understand until she was fifty-one that people send nonverbal communication signals with their eyes.

- Proxemic communication: He doesn't understand physical space communication, the subtle territorial cues and norms of personal boundaries. He may be an unwitting "space invader." The rules of proxemics not only vary from culture to culture, but from person to person depending upon relationship. Intimate? Casual but personal? Social only? Public space? For many kids with autism or Asperger's, deciphering proxemics requires an impossible level of inference.

There's no short cut or magic bullet to your child's becoming comfortable with social interaction. It takes practice, in-the-moment, get-messy, make-mistakes practice (emphasizing that "mistake" is just another word for "practice.") Unlike the idea that providing a language-rich environment will encourage language development, mainstreaming a child with her typically-developing peers will not bring forth improved social abilities without direct, concrete teaching of social concepts. Without this direct teaching, your child will still bob along into adulthood in

There's no short cut or magic bullet to your child's becoming comfortable with social interaction. It takes practice.

that same sea of social miscommunication. Teaching your child to be social is a mosaic of thousands upon thousands of petite learning opportunities and encounters that, properly channeled, will coalesce into a core of self-confidence. It requires you, as his parent, his teacher, his guide, to be socially aware 110% of the time, break down the web of social intricacies, clue him in to the social nuances that are so difficult for him to perceive, and do so in a way he can understand.

Social navigation is necessary at every turn in our lives: at home, at work, at school, in our travels about the community, in our shopping, recreation, and worship. As you shepherd your child through this challenging landscape, I implore you to do it without the mindset that he is "less than." Sending the child a constant message that he's inherently deficient will surely build the wall that prevents the progress we want. Self-esteem, an essential component of social functioning, will not flourish in an environment that sends the message that she's not good enough the way she is. Some of her behaviors may not be conducive to her social development, but always separate the behavior from the whole child.

With Bryce, I knew from the start that we were in for a long, long trek. On a good day, it meant the routine unfolded pleasantly and productively and we could see progress toward our goals. On a bad day, it meant living and coping not one day at a time, but one moment at a time. On one of those days when the road stretched too far ahead, I began to wonder, how much is enough? When the need is as all-encompassing and never-ending as is the constellation of social skills, how would I know where the teaching and nurturing of those skills would cross the line into repair mode? Where lay the boundary between providing my son the galaxy of services and opportunities he needed and, well, bombardment? Barely five years old, he put in rigorous six-hour days in a developmental kinder-garten with afternoon inclusion, speech therapy three days a week, adaptive PE, and one-on-one occupational therapy. Yes, we could go on making the rounds of after-school supplemental therapies, tutorings, and social activities. But I had serious misgivings about what sort of message it sent.

Something is wrong with me.

I recalled that first advice from our pediatrician, to trust my instincts, that I knew more than I thought I knew. I chose to follow that advice. I pulled Bryce out of everything but school. I did it because I believed the pace, the manner, and the context in which we taught him were parts of the skill-building equation as crucial as the skill itself. Force-feeding without creating relevance without building a framework for him to understand the why behind his social behavior would bring forth a gag response. The environment in which he would best be able to learn would not be one of incessant pressure and demand. My job was to create that foundation where social awareness could flourish and he could develop genuine self-esteem and be comfortable inside his own skin. With those underpinnings, I trusted that he would more easily learn social skills on his unique timetable, not one that I or others had lifted from books or charts or comparisons to other children. I wasn't sure I was doing the right thing, but with Bryce there did seem to be a direct relationship between the pace of teaching, his growing self-awareness, and his self-esteem. His down time was his recharging time. It enabled him to exercise some choice over a portion of his life and consequently, to be willing to give 100% at school. "Bravo," said his paraeducator. "You wouldn't believe how many exhausted kids I see. Like all kids, they need time to just be kids."

Bryce, who by thirteen had succeeded at social interaction in settings ranging from team sports to school dances, was a splendid example of what a child with autism can achieve when healthy self-esteem leads the way. How many, many miles along the spectrum we traveled to get there. In hindsight, I can see that my relentless reinforcing of his self-esteem proved an enormous factor in his willingness to be nudged out of his comfort zone, and to expand it.

Teaching social awareness is a step toward social competency. As an overall concept, it may feel overwhelming, but as with any large task, you'll be more effective if you separate and clarify your goals, address one goal at a time, start small, and build on incremental successes. Remove obstacles (usually sensory, language, or self-esteem issues) and throw out preconceived, stereotypical measures of what constitutes progress, the definition of which is sure to be a moving target.

Separating goals and keeping them manageable is of the essence, because where messages overlap, you can't expect your child to be able to sort the primary goal from the secondary one. If you want your child to be a pleasant, involved member of the family at dinner, recognize that several intersecting goals are involved. To isolate the social component, you may need to offer adaptive seating and utensils, eliminate foods (his and others'), smells and sounds that offend his senses, and make concerted efforts to include him in the conversation. Ensure that his time at the dinner table is not an exercise in unpleasant smells and enforced two-bite tastings, lectures about manners and the incomprehensible prattling of the group. If the goal is socialization, separate it from food goals or fine motor processing goals. I've had to walk that talk. At various times in my kids' lives, they ate breakfast in their bedrooms. The commotion of the morning routine rattled them, and the goal at that time of day was nutrition, not socialization. This temporary accommodation, one of many we made along the way, lasted a few months, not forever. And let me tell you where this patient separation of goals got us. The year Bryce was twelve, we celebrated my birthday as a family in one of the most elegant white-tablecloth restaurants in town. The boys loved it, and I will experience few moments more magical than watching Bryce stride confidently to the piano bar, five-dollar tip in hand to ask the piano man, "Could you please play 'Stardust' for my mom? It's her birthday." The many years of slow-but-steady acclimation melted away.

Social competence builds, phoenix-like, upon itself particle by particle, day by day. "To the top of the mountain, one step at a time," advises the old proverb. We're not Moses, so there won't be tablets at the summit—if there is a summit—but if there were they might look something like this:

1. Eradicate the thought of "fix."

2. Build your child's self-esteem as a foundation for social risk-taking and a shield against the unkindness of others.

3. Focus on social awareness, interpretation, and problem solving as the means to developing social skills. Learning to consider and interpret the thoughts and feelings of others and maintain a balance within social situations will smooth the way for generalization of skills across situations and settings.

4. Create circumstances in which she can practice social skills and succeed, not intermittently, not occasionally, but constantly.

5. Be specific in defining your social skill goals, and beware of goals that overlap or conflict.

6. Start at your child's real level of social processing, not a perceived or assumed one. Some of our kids with advanced vocabularies and elevated IQs fool us into thinking their social abilities are as developed. In most cases, they're not.

7. Keep teaching increments small. Build as you go.

8. Maintain an open-ended definition of what constitutes progress. Two steps forward/one step back is still growth to be celebrated.

9. Provide a reasonable out for social risk-taking situations. You want him to try the church choir or after-school Lego club or volunteering at the pet shelter, but if after several sessions he hates it, praise him for trying, affirm it's okay to stop, and move on to something else.

10. Remember that social rules and social expectations change over time and within contexts. A socially appropriate behavior for a child of five may be inappropriate for a teenager. What is okay in the school cafeteria may not be okay in a restaurant or when visiting someone's home.

Fitting into our social world requires a tremendous amount of effort on your child's part. He does the best he can with the abilities and social quotient he has. Despite the nuances he doesn't get, he does know when you believe in him and when that belief falters.

"To the top of the mountain, one step at a time." One of my son Connor's favorite children's books told the story of Sir Edmund Hillary and his Sherpa guide Tenzing Norgay, the first people to reach the summit of Mt. Everest. We talked about the controversy over the years regarding which one of them had put their foot on the top first. Amid speculation that Tenzing arrived at the summit a step or two ahead of the more famous Sir Edmund Hillary, Tenzing's son Jamling told *Forbes* magazine in 2001: "I did ask him, and he said, 'You know, it's not important, Jamling. We climbed as a team.'" Like Tenzing, you've been climbing this mountain for many years. Like Hillary, your child is making his first ascent. Be his Sherpa, knowing and helping him see that the view along the way can be spectacular.

Chapter Nine

Identify what triggers my meltdowns.

You call them meltdowns, to me they feel like blow-ups. They're more horrid for me than they are for you.

Everything I do is telling you something, when my words cannot, about how I'm reacting to what's happening around me, about the feelings of pain and panic happening inside me. I'm not "out to get you" and I can't "just stop." I melt down when one or more of my senses go into overload, or because I've been pushed past my ability to deal with the people and situation around me. And I might melt down because something feels wrong in my body, like allergies, or not sleeping well, or tummy troubles. Whatever it is, it feels like I'm being attacked.

I need you to help me stay out of situations that affect me that way. If you can figure out why I melt down, you can prevent it. I can't do that on my own. Look for signs, because they are always there, and I may not be able to tell you in words.

Here's something you may not believe but will by the end of this chapter: there can be innumerable reasons why a child with autism melts down, blows up, loses it, falls apart. Being bratty, petulant, obstinate, spoiled, or "not trying hard enough" is so far down the list of possibilities that I can't even see it without binoculars.

We've already faced the unvarnished bottom line: all behavior springs from a reason, and all behavior is communication. A meltdown is a clear message from a child who is not able to tell you in any other way that a situation has escalated beyond his point of self-regulation; something in his environment has caused his delicate neurology to go haywire and he can no longer manage it. It may seem to erupt "out of the blue," but in fact there were warning signs, clues—sometimes subtle but nevertheless there—that were either not recognized, disregarded or ignored. Even the child whose oral speech skills are adequate in an ordinary setting can lose his voice when under stress. For the limited-speech or nonspeaking child, there may be no choice other than behavior,

Remember, always, that it's not within his control. He doesn't make a conscious choice to melt down.

particularly if she's been taught no alternate functional communication system. Regardless of the child's speaking skills, it will be easier for you to keep your wits about you if you remember, always, that it's not within his control. He doesn't make a conscious choice to melt down. Thinking for even a moment that the child somehow wants the kind of negative attention he gets from a meltdown is illogical and counterproductive.

Square One for us has to be the belief that this child would interact appropriately if he could, but he has neither the social cognition, sensory processing abilities, nor expressive language to achieve it. If this isn't your current mindset, it may take conscious practice to get there. With practice, the assumption that there is a trigger, and the curiosity and tenacity to delve for it, can become second nature. Many other ideas we've discussed in this book come together here: sensory overload, can't versus won't, inadequate expressive speech, social processing challenges.

When I say all behavior has a reason, I mean an explanation, an underlying cause. Seeking out reasons can be laborious and challeng¬ing. It's not the same as making excuses for the behavior. An excuse is merely an attempt at justification, and may or may not have any truth behind it. Scrutinize these statements:

"He doesn't want to. He could (behave/sit still/cooperate) if he wanted to."

"She just has to try harder."

"I taught him but he won't do it."

See how these attitudes let us, as parents, teachers, or caregivers, off the hook, excuse us from the harder work of finding an underlying cause? How many, many times we've heard the cliché, "You can do anything if you want to badly enough." Right. That's why we know people who can time-travel, or live to be 300 years old. Can a blind child copy off the whiteboard, if he wants to badly enough? If that sounds familiar, good. Because we're back at Chapter Three, distinguishing between won't and can't, and echoing other chapters where we've suggested that how vehemently we—or a child—want(s) something isn't the test of whether it's possible, nor whether we or the child are capable of it. Lack of motivation isn't always the reason for noncompliance. All the motivation in the world may still require patient, sustained instruction and/or assistive technology. We can't (and won't) use "he just doesn't want to" as the rationalization for turning away from more arduous but more effective intervention.

As for "try harder," who will volunteer to step us and model for us how effective that is for changing a behavior with which you've repeatedly struggled (lose weight, save money, stop smoking, procrastinating, being late, biting nails, cut down on screen time)?

And "I taught him but he won't do it"? Remember that it isn't teaching if he didn't learn it. And he can't learn it unless you teach it in a manner comprehensible to him.

Many will be the wearying moment when the root cause of your child's meltdown won't be immediately evident. There may never be a time in your life when it's more incumbent upon you to become a detective, that is, to ascertain, become aware of, diagnose, discover, expose, ferret out. Baffling behaviors always have a root cause, and identifying them does require that you be detailed, curious, and thorough in your search for that cause. You must be biology detective, psychology sleuth, and environmental investigator.

Most meltdown triggers cluster into several areas. If you can pinpoint the trigger, you can prevent the meltdown rather than trying to interrupt or extinguish it once it's in progress (rarely possible). Think of the old Chinese adage: give a man a fish and he eats for a day; teach him how to fish and he eats for a lifetime. Your ability to identify your child's triggers is the first step in helping him identify them himself. Self-regulation can follow.

Let's look at four trigger clusters.

- Sensory overload
- Physical/physiological triggers
  - Food allergies or sensitivities

- • Sleep disturbances

- • Gastrointestinal problems

- • Inadequate nutrition

- • Biochemical imbalances

- • Unarticulated illness or injury

- Emotional triggers

  - • Frustration

  - • Disappointment

  - • Maltreatment

  - • Sense of unfairness

- Poor examples from adults

Sensory overload

As discussed throughout this book, always look for sensory issues first.

When Bryce was three, we celebrated my birthday at a relative's home, a familiar place to him. Halfway through the evening he began to career through the house in agitation, and when I attempted to calm him with measures that usually worked, he fought it, arms lashing wildly. Time to go, too soon, but that's the way it was. I gathered coats and toys. "Wait," said a usually understanding relative. "Are you going to let a three-year-old dictate the evening to the rest of the family?" I knew what he meant. He wanted me to enjoy the evening and the special attention he felt I deserved. But yes, the three-year-old's needs would detour the evening. It didn't negate that we had a lovely time up to that point. And no, he wasn't dictating. He was communicating. Because his spoken language wasn't there yet, I had to search for meaning in his behavior. The aggression drained out of him as soon as we left. He hadn't been acting out of petulance. He had been in pain.

The crux of this story is, I knew something was hurting him. It never occurred to me that he would try to ruin my evening. That made no sense. Developmentally, he didn't yet have the ability to form that level of deliberate intent. He was in a familiar place with people he knew, loved, and normally enjoyed. Clearly, something was amiss. Too much unfiltered noise? A different, queasy-inducing smell? Overtired, too many people? I didn't know and it didn't matter in that moment. The most important thing was to end the discomfort before it became the last thing he remembered and the first thing he associated with that venue in the future.

Physical/physiological triggers

- **Food allergies and intolerances/sensitivities**

These terms are sometimes used interchangeably, but they're not the same thing. An allergy is an abnormally acute immune-system response. An intolerance (sometimes called nonallergic hypersensitivity) is a drug-like reaction to a substance, the degree of response to which varies from person to person (e.g., two red jelly beans may incite hyper or aggressive behavior in one child, whereas another may be able to tolerate a handful). Plenty of evidence exists that both can cause aggressive, belligerent or moody behavior in children. The list of possible offending substances includes anything that goes into the mouth. Common culprits are food dyes, preservatives and other additives, milk, nuts, strawberries, citrus, shellfish, eggs, wheat, corn, and soy.

To detect a substance that may be affecting your child's behavior, keep a food diary of everything he eats for a week, noting times when behaviors occur. If you see a pattern of problematic behavior after the lunchtime peanut butter sandwich, consider eliminating wheat or nuts from your child's diet for two weeks. Eliminate one substance at a time; phase it out slowly if it's a favorite. Did behaviors diminish after elimination of the food? Test your results by reintroducing a small amount of the food, gradually increasing the dose, seeing if and at what point the behavior returns.

- **Sleep disturbances**

Behavior problems are sure to follow the child who's chronically exhausted. If you've already tried the usual tactics—setting an inviolable bedtime routine, elimination of naps, "spraying for monsters," avoiding overstimulation—consider our now-familiar nemesis, sensory problems. Could it be:

  - Noisy clocks, furnaces, or plumbing? Weather noises such as gurgling gutters, branches scraping against window or roof?

  - Scratchy sheets, blankets, or pajamas? New items? They can feel and smell wrong, especially if you've taken away an old favorite. Consider that the "right" size pajamas might be a size larger (less constricting) or smaller (comforting pressure) than what she's wearing, and that comfortable nightwear is a very personal preference and isn't limited to conventional pajamas.

  - Competing smells of laundry products and toiletries?

  - Proprioceptive insecurity? She may feel lost in space in

106

her bed. A mummy-style sleeping bag, guardrail, tent or canopy with privacy curtains might help.

- **Gastrointestinal problems**

For reasons not fully understood, autistic children seem to experience a higher than typical instance of misery-inducing gastrointestinal problems. Your child may be voicing her pain through extreme behavior. Acid reflux (heartburn) can cause esophageal pain, sleep disruption and abdominal discomfort. Constipation and its complications (impaction, encopresis), diarrhea and chronic flatulence have social as well as physiological implications. More serious illnesses such as Crohn's disease, ulcerative colitis, and irritable bowel syndrome (IBS) require ongoing medical supervision. The nonspeaking or minimally speaking child's inability to articulate her discomfort or cooperate with typical testing are reasons why many children go undiagnosed.

- **Inadequate nutrition**

At the dawn of the computer age, the acronym GIGO arose, meaning garbage in, garbage out. It's not just for programmers. A child may be eating a lot of food, but if it's of low nutritive value, his brain may be starving, acutely affecting his behavior. One way to improve nutrition is to choose foods closer to their original condition. Processed white flour and white sugar products, processed meats, soda, and fruit-flavored drink products are nutrient-low while high in fat, salt, sugar, and chemicals. If behavior deteriorates early in the day, could skipping breakfast be the culprit?

As with allergy identification, make dietary changes s-l-o-w-l-y. A one-fell-swoop wipeout of your child's favorite foods is a guaranteed recipe for failure.

107

- **Biochemical imbalances**

This can include anything and everything: too much/not enough stomach acid, bile irregularities, vitamin or mineral deficiencies, yeast or bacterial imbalance. It may manifest as anxiety, depression, aggression, weight fluctuations, sleep problems, phobias, and skin problems.

- **Unarticulated illness or injury**

Ear infections, tooth and gum problems, and broken bones are examples of excruciatingly painful conditions that may be impossible for a child with limited verbal ability to adequately communicate.

Emotional triggers

- **Frustration**

Frustration comes when she's trying but not able to meet your (or her own) expectations and goals. Maybe she doesn't understand the expectation, or maybe it's too high, unachievable. Maybe it's achievable but she doesn't understand why it's necessary or relevant, or maybe she doesn't have the social, motor, or language skills to accomplish it.

I'll never forget a story I heard years ago about a whirling dervish of a girl with ADHD, nine years old. Her teacher proposed a deal, a reward for meeting a behavioral goal. If the girl could "be good" for three weeks, the teacher would buy her an ice cream cone. The girl reported to her therapist: "Is she kidding? I don't even know what 'be good' means. I can't 'be good' for three hours, let alone three weeks. And besides, I don't like ice cream."

Identify what triggers my meltdowns.

The goal: unrealistic, out of reach.

Specific definition of the goal: none.[2]

Guidance offered to help in accomplishing the goal: none.

The reward: irrelevant, and nowhere near equal in value to the effort required.

Here's a scenario six times more constructive: Teacher and student (1) meet one-on-one and (2) discuss and agree to (3) a specific, (4) short-range goal (5) that is achievable and (6) has a meaningful motivator as a reward. For instance, the student will work toward remaining in her seat or other designated spot (her sensory needs may be better met, and she may be better able to comply if standing at a podium, lying full length on a mat, or sinking into a bean bag) during silent reading time, which is the twenty minutes following lunch recess (short period of time following a physical-release outlet offers best chance of success). She'll start with five-minute increments and work up from there. Success will earn her a token toward computer time, a movie pass, or other mutually-agreed-upon end result that's attractive to her.

For most children, experiencing success results in positive momentum. As her successes build, her frustration will ebb, and so will the upsetting outbursts.

---

2. The goal was for the student to "be good." How is a child to infer what we mean by "good" when it may be the most subjective word in the English language? It's an adjective, a noun, an interjection, an adverb. Dictionary.com cites *fifty-nine* definitions and sub-definitions. "Good" is a moving target that changes from venue to venue, relationship to relationship, situation to situation. It changes with the time of day and it changes as the child ages. "Be good" isn't an achievable goal unless the specific actions needed to fulfill "good" are spelled out to the child in a manner she can comprehend and attain.

- **Disappointment**

Disappointment comes when someone a child counted upon didn't come through; an event anticipated didn't happen. While a typically-developing child may be able to adapt easily when schedules or events change, the child with autism depends upon routine and familiarity. Accommodating abrupt changes of direction in his day requires skills he may not yet have and can cause disruption from which it can take hours to recover. Disappointment is a matter of degree for every individual, and it may take concerted effort to fully understand, accept, and empathize with your child's perspective. To you, it's a blip in the routine. To him, it's a malevolent threat to emotional equilibrium. Disappointments may be unpredictable: the store is out of his favorite juice, the usual route to school is detoured because of road repair, his TV show is preempted for a breaking news report, a play date is cancelled because Addie is sick. Others can be circumvented with forethought and planning. Tell him the pool at this year's vacation hotel will not have a diving board and show him a picture from the hotel brochure or website. Have Grandma tell him she will be serving apple pie instead of pumpkin at Thanksgiving this year. Explain that Calvin the beloved Camp Counselor won't be back this year but go to meet Nathan the New Guy before the session starts.

- **Maltreatment**

She's being attacked, provoked, or teased by peers, siblings, or other adults, in person or through emails, texts, posts, other media, other avenues we haven't yet imagined at this writing. Whether in your home, your school, or any other setting, there's only one acceptable position: 100% unacceptable. How user-friendly is your child's environment in this regard? Your autistic child has neither the verbal sophistication nor the social acuity to adequately defend herself. Meltdowns are only the beginning. Close on their heels may be anxiety, depression, and chronic fatigue. Taking action to protect your child or student in such situations is mandatory.

At the elementary school my children attended, the administration and teaching staff fero¬ciously enforced a policy declaring the school a No Put-Down Zone, dealing with incidences of unkindness in any degree promptly and decisively. We never took our school's policy for granted, not for a minute. At another school, a mother told me a different story:

Just because he can't tell you it's happening doesn't mean that it isn't.

> My son started first-grade with positive, consistent feedback from us, but quickly deteriorated under daily physical abuse from his peers. Both the teacher and the principal reacted to my repeated concerns by admonishing me to stop being overprotective. My son needed to learn how to take care of himself; these things happen between kids and you can't always be there to save them. He needed to learn to stand up for himself, stop being such a baby, focus more, work harder, listen better, do as told, try harder, be more responsive, and on, and on, and on.

I crumble inside every time I hear a shameful account such as this one. "These things happen between kids"? Of course they do, when the adults in charge continue to allow it. Whether the perpetrators are peers, siblings, or adults, our declining to take action declares our choice to allow harassment to flourish. And if the victim responds with anger or aggression, we can't feign surprise or indignation.

So here's the chant again: just because he can't tell you it's happening doesn't mean that it isn't. Most harassment happens out of the hearing range of parents, teachers, and other adults: on the bus, in the bathroom, in the halls, on the playground. Teach your child or student, as soon as he's able, to 1) protest appropriately, "Stop! I don't like that," and 2) tell a trusted adult. And know that your radar has to be up at all times. If you sense something, say something.

- **Sense of unfairness**

"Fair" is one of those hazy, imprecise terms perplexing to our autistic kids. He doesn't think in terms of fair or unfair, but does know he's having trouble balancing his needs with the rules. Adults often think *fair* means impartial, equitable, unbiased. Family rules, school rules, and team rules apply to each sibling, student, or teammate equally. But autism un-levels the playing field. It potholes the field. All things are not equal. So our thinking on the subject of *fair* must change. Here it is:

Fair doesn't mean everything is equal.

Fair is when everyone gets what they need.

Poor examples from adults

I once worked for a general manager who would occasionally invoke an indelicate metaphor when he wanted to place responsibility in someone else's lap. He didn't care for the usual sports idioms like "the ball is in their court." Rather, he liked to "put the turd back in their pocket." Vivid, unpleasant imagery, but sometimes that's what it takes to focus attention on something from which we'd rather turn away.

The mirror can be unforgiving, but any examination of our child's undesirable behavior has to start with a look at our own. "Speak when you are angry and you will make the best speech you'll ever regret," said Laurence J. Peter, author of *The Peter Principle: Why Things Always Go Wrong*. If you react with anger and frustration to your child or student's meltdowns, you're modeling the very behavior you want him or her to change. It's incumbent upon you as an adult to refrain from responding in kind. Be your own behavior detective. Figure out what triggers your own boiling point and interrupt the episode before you reach that point. When you feel your emotional thermostat rising, better to temporarily remove yourself from the situation. Tell your child, "You're angry [frustrated, upset] and I am, too. I need to be by myself for a few minutes so I can calm down. I am going to my room [or outside or upstairs] for now, but I will come back to you and we can talk about it."

Be aware of the many ways in which we unwittingly make a bad situation worse.

- We respond with derision—mocking or laughing at someone's pain or misfortune, projecting a serves-you-right attitude.

- We sometimes make unfair, irrel¬evant comparisons, such as "Your sister never did this."

- We launch into kitchen-sink arguments, bringing up bygone incidents: "This is just like the time you _____."

- We may make unproven accusations: "You must have done this. Nobody else would have."

- We raise the pitch or volume of our voice, so that all the child hears is our tone, not the words. (Think of the humorous-but-true comeback, "If I shout at you in French, will you become fluent?")

- We set double standards, holding an autistic child to a different set of rules than peers or siblings.

As with any difficult situation, planning is key. At a time when you're calm, think through how you can better handle the next incident. Then write down your plan, keep it in an accessible place, and refer to it periodically to keep it fresh in your mind. Role play it to the bathroom mirror. See what your face and actions communicate, along with your words.

"How much more grievous are the consequences of anger than the causes of it," said first-century Roman educator Marcus Aurelius. From time to time, a parent will tell me, with strident conviction, that hitting their child was the only way to get through to him or her, and that it worked because the child "turned out okay." I can't begin to understand what "turned out okay" means when the child in question has yet to reach adulthood, or even adolescence. I hear such behavior called spanking, swatting, paddling, or corporal punishment, but by any name, it's an aggressive act perpetrated almost invariably in anger. Sometimes it happens in a momentary loss of self-control, sometimes with the mistaken conviction that it will somehow, without the effort of instruction, teach appropriate behavior.

An angry physical response doesn't teach a child what he did wrong, doesn't teach him what to do or the skills needed to do it, doesn't foster the mutual respect and understanding necessary to a trusting relationship. It confronts him with a double standard he can't possibly understand—it's okay for adults to behave aggressively with children but not for him to behave in kind, to anyone. The least consequence this will create is discord. At its worst, the discord will lead to distrust and disconnect. We've just discussed the importance of teaching a child to report maltreatment to a trusted adult. Trust isn't an entitlement a child owes the authority figures in his life. It must be earned, and once earned, maintained on a daily basis. Whatever actions you must take or refrain from, you want to be one of those trusted adults in a child's life, because if you're not, the horrifying long-term consequence is that he may not tell you if, in the future, another adult (or peer) behaves aggressively or abusively toward him.

Anger is contagious, and in the end, it costs us: in time lost, energy expended, trust violated, self-worth stunted, feelings wounded, and long-term results unattained. Yet, anger is inevitable in the human experience. Learning to handle anger with proactive self-control and dignity ultimately empowers both you and, through your example, your child.

Ferreting out the causes and consequences of troubling behaviors has a formal name. A Functional Behavior Analysis (FBA) assesses specific behaviors based on their ABCs: the antecedent (cause or trigger), the behavior itself, and the consequence (what happens to the child as a result of the behavior). An FBA can be a formal process carried out in the school setting by trained personnel or an informal one, i.e., parental home observation. The idea behind an FBA is that, once identified, the antecedents and consequences of a behavior can be altered or modified by teaching the child more appropriate behavior.

That's such an important piece of the equation that I'm going to repeat it: behavior change doesn't stop at interrupting or extinguishing an undesirable behavior. However baffling or distasteful to you, a child's behavior happens for a reason and fills a need. Squelching a behavior without uncovering and addressing the underlying cause will only result in another behavior rising to fill the need.

Learning to deal with your child's meltdowns isn't easy. But answers await those who are up for the hunt. I found the process wondrous. The better I got at identi¬fying and respecting Bryce's triggers, the more peaceful life became. The frightening several-times-a-day meltdowns diminished to several times a week, morphed briefly into occasional passive-aggressive responses, then vanished completely. Completely. Before long, I didn't think about it in any manner other than being grateful for how we faced down something so ugly and overcame it. My recall of those difficult times faded with every passing year. It's one of the most impressive special effects I've ever seen.

Chapter Ten

Love me without "if."

When I hear things like, "If you would just—," and "Why can't you—?", I feel your disappointment in me already. And it makes me wonder: did you do every last thing your parents and teachers expected of you? I bet you didn't, and I bet you wouldn't like being reminded of it all the time.

I didn't choose to have autism. Remember that it's happening to me, not you. I think a lot about growing up, things I want to be, things I want to do. It scares me that without your help, I may never do those things.

I need you to be my rock, my defender, my guide. Can you love me for who I am, without any "if" or "but"? Then we'll see how far I can go!

"The difference between heaven and earth is not so much altitude but attitude."

These words, from the book *The Power of Unconditional Love* by Ken Keys, Jr., form the overarching sentiment for everything I believe about raising an autistic child, and they come from a man who lived that difference every day. Polio put Keys in a wheelchair the last fifty years of his life, so he knew a little about living with a disability. It didn't stop him from writing fifteen books about loving life, finding happiness in what you already have, and keeping your focus forward. Unconditional love, he contends, is based on dualities, the most encompassing of which is that to love someone else, we have to love ourselves, "accepting all parts of ourselves." What better example to set for your child?

Unconditional love, to which you attach no "if" or "but" qualifiers, is both magical and attainable. No question, the challenges of raising atypical children can be staggering. Face in the dirt, knife in the heart, down for the count. Rising above and firmly pushing aside our own fears, disappointments, expectations, and lost dreams can seem like a mission of overwhelming enormity. Your child's limitations become yours—the places you can't take him, the social settings he can't handle, the people he can't relate to, the food he won't eat. Yeah, it can be a long list. But it has always been my cherished privilege to claim our two boys as mine and to love them unconditionally. It's taught me profound lessons about how excruciat¬ing it can be to keep that kind of love in the crosshairs at all times.

It takes courage to admit you're scared, feel cheated, heartsick, depleted. Wanting out of that matrix and not knowing how to start. Here's how: by knowing you can do this. It's already in you.

In the early days of contemplating what Bryce's life and my family's would be like with autism in our midst, I couldn't deny that it could be much worse. All around me were people who had confronted just that. Close friends had lost their precious two-year-old daughter to a heart defect, a life-shattering event far more devastating than anything autism threw at our family. It underscored the price-lessness of what we had—hope. "To travel hopefully," Robert Louis Stevenson wrote in 1881, "is a better thing than to arrive."

Bryce taught me that happiness doesn't come from getting what you want, but from wanting what you already have. It's the greatest gift I have ever been given. A friend once asked me, how do you get there? What do you think is the secret of your success?

It's no secret. It's just this: accept your situation without bitterness. Play the cards you drew with grace and optimism. Bitterness can be a formidable foe; overcoming it can be a daily exercise. Some of us make it, some of us don't.

Back in Chapter Three, I spoke of a parent who claimed that because of autism, he couldn't have a relationship with his son. He knew his son would end up in jail. I talked and reasoned and pleaded away the afternoon with this man, begging him to see he was setting up a self-fulfilling prophecy. Couldn't he take one baby step out, imagining a different outcome for his belligerent but bright child—ten minutes of floor time, coming to school once a month, finding a restaurant they both liked? I think he loved his son but to the child it no doubt felt conditional, dependent upon a certain kind of behavior, even if there were organic reasons why he couldn't comply. In the end, they both lost out. This dad couldn't move beyond his bitterness and grief.

Grief is real, autism is real, and many parents go through a grief process upon learning their child has autism. Getting stuck in that grief—that's the true tragedy, not that your child has autism.

A few years ago, I spotted a short article about a mom of an autistic five-year-old and a behavior therapist who had launched an autism center offering consultative services for custom home programs, family support, and training. *Oh, happy day,* I thought, until the next sentence put a pin in my balloon. A local business owner had stepped up to donate a portion of sales to this promising new venture. "We wanted to help," he said. "Autism is a tragedy for families."

> **One of the greatest tragedies that can befall a child with autism is to be surrounded by adults who think it's a tragedy.**

It goes without saying that we deeply appreciate the support, financial and emotional, of our local communities. But I cannot say this more strongly: what you see is what you get. Autism is a tragedy for families only if they allow it to be. And one of the greatest tragedies that can befall a child with autism is to be surrounded by adults who think it's a tragedy.

Try to imagine yourself in the world of your child or student, with its incessant sensory invasion, eddies of incomprehensible language swirling around him, the impatience and disregard of "normal" people. You face the same question I did so many long years ago. If I did not swallow my own anguish and be the one to step up for my son, who would? And if not now, when?

Do you dare imagine your child's life as an adult after you're gone? Over the years, parents of autistic children have let me know that this is indisputably the question that terrifies them most. It's a harsh question, and the one that keeps me on track every day of my life. What kind of life awaits an adult who has limited language ability, doesn't comprehend the law and law enforcement, the banking system, public transportation, workplace issues such as punctuality, basic etiquette, respectful communication, group dynamics? To what level of quality can life rise without at least a few meaningful interpersonal relationships, meaningful work, meaningful pastimes or hobbies? Most children grow up assuming these things will be the components of their adult lives. For the child with autism, such a future can exist, but not without the collaborative intervention of adults committed 100% to the idea that to have the opportunities to be everything one can be, and be happy with themselves, is the birthright of every child. It's through unconditional love we teach our children to be functional and comfortable within their autism, not to replicate so-called typical children.

For some cosmic, not-to-be-understood reason, I was blessed with the serenity to bypass the denial and the anger and the self-pity that frequently come unbidden and unwelcome when we learn our child has a disability. This wasn't a superpower and I'm no supermom. I endured—and still endure—bouts with melancholy and self-doubt, and I still fall prey to what I call the Knife-to-the-Heart moments. These are the times when the rest of the world seems intent on letting you know your child is different and apart. Often there's no conscious malice; it happens because the mainstream population is going about their business in mainstream fashion, which doesn't or can't include your child. Other times, the spite is intentional—the child-cruel remark, the birthday party everyone else is invited to, the snubs on the bus. Then come the questions he asks you as he begins to figure out that he's different. I thought if I endured enough Knife-to-the-Heart moments, I would develop scar tissue or the ability to laugh them off. I haven't. But as both my boys moved with increasing grace toward maturity and independence, those moments became fewer, farther between and more fleeting. The power they hold over me weakened over time.

Loving Bryce unconditionally required making peace with what sometimes seemed like reduced opportunities. As a young child, he didn't seem to want conventional friendships, play dates and sleepovers, wasn't interested in the usual after-school activities like soccer or choir. He couldn't tolerate large-scale shows or sporting events in arenas or stadiums. Travel had to be carefully orchestrated. Curiously, I can't say I missed these things because he was a happy child who seemed comfortable with himself. Still, I pondered. And still I asked a lot of questions.

My children's middle school years arrived, and there I sat one morning in our psychologist's office, bewildered yet again at my son's social development, which seemed to meander all over the landscape without ever treading the established path. During this meeting, after the practical and the actionable suggestions, the psychologist gave me this memorable advice: "And remember: all children, all people, unfold in their own time. This may not be his time. His time will come."

We gave (and still give) Bryce the time and space to do that. Those times did come. His social, academic and recreational accomplishment came right on time—his time. It may have been a few years behind the typical timeline, but he did them as successfully as many kids, teens, and adults, and what's more, the minute he did, we often magically forgot he ever hadn't.

Every day of Bryce's childhood, I told him he was an interesting and wonderful person and I was the luckiest mommy who ever lived. In the beginning, I believed it enough to start saying it, but as time went on a marvelous thing happened. It became fact to me. I began to actively look for things about him to articulate. I told him I was proud of how readily he shared treats and privileges with others, how I admired his devotion to his school work, how

I enjoyed the clever associations he made as he pulled minute details out of movies and related them to his real life. How I could trust him because he never lied, how well he took care of himself with healthy food, hygiene, and sleep choices. In time, it became part and parcel of his self-image. And because he believed it, he grew into a young man with remarkable aplomb, self-confidence, empathy and work ethic.

Think of it as affirmative brainwashing. The more you articulate your child's strengths and gifts, the more both of you grow to believe it.

If you can get to a place where you believe, accept, and put true unconditional love into practice, you'll find yourself infused with a commanding energy on behalf of your child. Without it, you're going to be running this race with a nasty pebble in your shoe. It may be a hundred-dollar shoe, but that pebble will ensure your focus dwells on the ever-more-painful wound to your extremity, rather than on the span of the road ahead or the beauty of your surroundings. It's a simple choice: let the irritant remain until it cripples you, or remove it and head for the horizon. With the full force of your commitment as the wind at your back, your child's time will come.

The fast track, record pace, maximum velocity, instant gratification culture of the twenty-first century is not the hand your child drew. He or she beckons you down that road less traveled, the road the poet Frost tells us is "just as fair, and having perhaps the better claim." It is perhaps the better claim because, at the end of this book, we have come full circle, back to where we started: neither you nor he yet know what the scope of his achievement can be. We can't see the end of the road, not only because it's full of steep climbs, dark puddles, downgrades, and tricky curves, but because there is no end. An energizing, uplifting thought, or a draining, wearying one—your choice. Henry Ford succeeded in spectacular fashion because he sought out people "who have an infinite capacity to not know what can't be done."

I want to leave you with the wise words of Joshua Liebman's "A Parent's Commandments." Our family committed to these directives at the naming ceremonies we held for both our sons shortly after their births, joyful occasions during which everything seemed possible for them. We could never have imagined how prescient these words would be:

> Give your child unconditional love, a love that
> is not dependent on report cards, clean hands or
> popularity.
>
> Give your child a sense of your whole-hearted
> acceptance, acceptance of his human frailties as
> well as his abilities and virtues.
>
> Give him a sense of truth; make him aware of
> himself as a citizen of the universe in which
> there are many obstacles as well as fulfillments.
>
> Give your child permission to grow up and
> make his own life independent of you.
>
> These are the laws of honoring your child.

Please join me in doing this for your child.

Along your road less traveled, it will make all the difference.

The Sum of *Ten Things*: Your Power of Choice

A. Overwhelmed

B. Paralyzed

C. Crushed

D. Scared

E. All of the above

These evocative words embody some of the first emotions to erupt in many parents of children newly diagnosed with autism. And no wonder, as we confront the sheer volume and weight of the decisions we now face and the bewildering range of choices within each decision, on subjects unfamiliar and unnerving. As time goes on, we find that the demands of having to make such choices never ends. Our child develops, matures, outgrows choices and solutions that once worked, faces new challenges requiring us to search out or create new alternatives.

We fear making the wrong choices.
It's like a never-ending multiple-choice test.

Do we find those choices empowering—or overpowering? Rare is the parent of an autistic child who hasn't at least once felt strapped to a pendulum reaching one of its polar apexes of too many choices, or no choices. This uncomfortable dichotomy leads to the same need—a way to make choices in which we can feel confident. Although we know intellectually there are no perfect parents, and that missteps are inevitable, we may also feel we simply can't make mistakes, that there is too much at risk. *We fear making the wrong choices.*

It's like a never-ending multiple-choice test.

After guiding two sons on the spectrum to adulthood, I grow light-headed trying to visualize a number that would approximate the decisions I've faced through the years, the incalculable choices I've considered. How many zeroes after the "1," how many miles long the roll of paper to write out such a number? I made those decisions in a kaleidoscope of modes—some instinctively, some carefully reasoned, some what the heck chances. Some with excitement, some with sadness. Some with gritted teeth, some with cautious hopefulness. A few of them brilliant from every facet, ranking at the top of what I consider the best decisions of my life.

The profusion of choices we must make can indeed be paralyzing. With our newly-diagnosed child, we enter a world of therapies, treatments, educational interventions, dietary considerations and home modifications that can feel like bombardment. We want to read everything, talk to everyone, try everything. We want to get up to speed immediately, without even knowing what speed might be the right speed, or in which direction we should travel.

How well I remember the urgency I felt in that first year after Bryce's autism diagnosis, trying to absorb all I needed to know about sensory integration, language processing, echolalia, fine motor development, social processing, motor planning, elimination diets, and on and on. I went to preschools, kindergartens and elementary schools for innumerable meetings that I came to think of as The Ol' Seven-on-One, folding and pleating myself into a kiddie-sized chair across the table from a platoon of professionals who each had a piece of my child's development (ergo, future) in their hands. Special educator, general education teacher, occupational therapist, speech therapist, adapted physical education specialist, psychologist, district autism specialist. They each brought sheaves of charts, numbers, opinions and observations specific to their knowledge and skill set.

How grateful I was for the abundance of what they were offering to my child! But in the depths of my most exhausted moments, I thought how much simpler it was for them, having to focus on only one area in which they were highly trained, for a fraction of the hours in a day, and a fraction of the days in a year. I, on the other side of the diminutive table under which I scraped and bruised my knees and my self-confidence, struggled to become instantly competent and conversant in all seven areas (not to mention the ones I didn't yet know about). I needed to be able to ask the questions that would allow me to best evaluate my son's Big Picture, every hour of every day. Within each of the seemingly limitless areas in which his autism affected his development, I had to be able to identify the broadest range of choices open to us if I was to make the best decisions possible. My older son's ADHD presented a different set of challenges seen from a different set of chairs across from a different set of players, but demanded no less in the way of cogent decision-making.

As my sons grew older, the dinky chairs gave way to larger versions in middle and high school, but the pace and breadth of decision-making didn't let up. And it became more complex as each child drew ever closer to adulthood and the stakes grew ever higher. Where once I had made all the decisions on their behalves, each passing year tipped the proportion of decision-making a bit more in their direction. The closer they drew to maturity, the more critical it became that they be able to shoulder a larger share of the decision-making, that they learn to articulate their needs and identify the choices therein. The ability to do so, to be an effective self-advocate, would make or break their success as adults. It wasn't enough that I knew how to identify and analyze choices. I had to teach my sons to do so, in increments manageable to them, in a manner that made sense to them.

Fight or flight? Some parents facing (or fleeing) this avalanche of choice will search for the nearest escape route, and they'll easily find it. They can choose to allow others to make the many decisions necessary about their child's education and health. Absent parent input, school personnel will make decisions about a child based on many factors, some with heartfelt effort to act in the best interests of the child, some with expediency or cost-efficiency as the primary motivation. Parents can make the choice to accept without question the recommendations of educators, therapists and clinicians, regardless of whether the advice is acutely individual to the child's needs, or generalized practices and treatments ("this is how we do it for all autistic kids").

But most parents and guardians I've encountered choose fight over flight. They step up to take the responsibility and the lead in making these choices. They recognize that in the ever-changing array of professionals in their child's life, parent/guardian stands as the constant. Teachers turn over annually, doctors and therapists change, caregivers, counselors and coaches come and go. It falls to the parent/guardian to act as Information Central, to ensure that the aggregate knowledge and wisdom, the sum of the choices we've made for and about our child, passes firmly into the hands of those who will play roles in the next chapter of his life and who will shape the next round of choices we must make. We often hear the metaphor that autism parenting is a marathon, not a sprint. I used that metaphor myself, for years, until I came to view it as much as a long-distance relay as a marathon. My nephew, having run both, describes it like this:

In a marathon, you fall into a comfortable rhythm and it's over in a few hours. The night before and the night of the race, you sleep in a nice bed. Contrast that to a 200-mile relay during which runners grab an hour or two's sleep in a van, on a gym floor, under a tree in a park. It's hours of cramped travel, then hours of waiting to leapfrog your teammates to the next point where you take off running.

You run much faster in a relay than in a marathon. You run in the dark over unfamiliar roads lit only by a headlamp. Various members of the team at various times argue about money and who's responsible for bringing what resources to the table. Some teammates think only of themselves and define their contribution without regard to the effect it has on other members of the team. During the race, unforeseen detours force some members to run farther than they had planned to complete their leg of the journey.

Sound familiar? The job of raising a child with autism is more like running a relay than a marathon. We remain as team captain, but every year we hand off our child to new teachers, and along the way we pass the figurative baton to new clinicians, new caregivers.

The ever-changing dynamics of the journey mean that choice, that weight swinging from the pivot point of the pendulum, can arc from feeling empowered to feeling overcome by endless, numberless choices. Sometimes we can't see the forest *or* the trees.

"I had no choice."

When I hear this declaration from parents, it's usually tinged with dejection, often fueled by melancholy, fear, anger. I just did an Internet search for the phrase and got 23 million results. That's a lot of anguish, desperation, bleakness. It can swamp us when we reach junctures where we feel we have no choice but to take action against our schools, leave spouses/partners, cut off family members, resort to medication. Or we simply take no action because we feel we have no choices. (Doing nothing is a choice. Sometimes it may even be a sound choice.)

The feeling of having no choice can be as immobilizing as having too many choices. And when I search the Internet for "I always have choices," I get only 62,000 results, a tiny fraction of the "no choice" population.

When we say we have no choice, we most often mean we have no palatable choices. No attractive or appealing choices. No acceptable or practical choices. Or that we've exhausted all the choices we've been able to identify.

But crummy choices are choices nonetheless. Here's an example. A common no-choice conundrum for parents of autistic children is the family member or members who do not—choose not to—understand autism's effect on the child. They often voice strident criticism of behaviors, impatience with sensory challenges, refusal to modify methods of communication or to otherwise accommodate and respect the child's needs. "We have a few family members who crush my son's self-esteem every time they are around him," a parent will tell me. "My only choice is to ease them out of our lives, quietly."

Seldom is the instance in which we truly have no choices.

This parent's choice is understandable, justifiable and even logical. But it is by far not the only choice. S/he could also choose to:

- Confront family members aggressively. "Your refusal to accept how Ben's autism affects him is damaging him, therefore we will allow you no further contact with him."

- Confront family members firmly but evenly. "I am sure you love Ben, but I don't think you realize how much your constant criticism hurts him. Until you can respect how Ben's autism affects him, it's in his best interest that he not be around you."

- Continue to attend family gatherings and confront each instance separately. "That's the second time in fifteen minutes you've criticized Ben for something he can't control. If you do it again, we will leave immediately."

- Take the passive-aggressive approach, cutting off contact with no explanation or communication.

- Ask a sympathetic family member to intervene with the offending members.

- Ask family members to attend family counseling.

- Ask family members to accept information about Ben's autism from a professional, such as his doctor, teacher or therapist.

- Ask the offending family members to propose a solution. "I can't allow your continued put-downs of Ben. What actions are you willing to take to change things?"

With a little brainstorming, the "only choice" becomes "many choices." Seldom is the instance in which we truly have no choices.

"If you limit your choices only to what seems possible or reasonable, you disconnect yourself from what you truly want, and all that is left is a compromise," warns author and composer Robert Fritz. Our fear of making the wrong choices often hovers over us with the menace of storm clouds, threatening to drown our well-being and leave us as the sodden pulp of despair. We turn away from the full range of choices when we do not like the choices. And indeed it will sometimes be true that all the choices will be abysmal. But learning to recognize the full range of choices available in any situation builds our confidence that we can make the right choices, even from a slate of options that forces us to hold our noses.

And that ability to constantly evaluate and choose gives us ultimate control over our lives. We lose a large part of our fear of making poor choices when we realize that the consequences of most choices aren't unalterable. We make the best choices we can with the resources available to us in that moment. The moment is ever-changing and so are many of our choices. Because of this, we can carry with us the assurance that regardless of how difficult the decision of the moment, *the way things are today does not have to be the way things are tomorrow.*

What could be a more inspiring thought than that?

My children's autism and ADHD endowed them with brains that learned differently than so-called typical children. For the most part, we enjoyed amicable and productive relationships with our schools, but we nearly always parted ways on one subject—testing. I railed against tests so poorly written they amounted to the equivalent of a foreign language to my autistic son. I threw them back at the schools, noting how riddled they were with obscure vocabulary that exceeded grade level, garbled facts, irrelevant distractions. "Plays into every weakness my students have," fumed one special educator who agreed with me. "Test" became a dirty four-letter word in our house, our own personal profanity.

So was it ironic or was it serendipitous and redemptive that what crystalized my thoughts on the power of choice came to me in the form of ... a test preparation handout? One fine day during Bryce's second year of college, an instructor distributed a sheet of tips and strategies for passing a multiple-choice test. I gave it a once-over and drew the parallel immediately: Parenting a child with autism is like having to pass an everlasting multiple-choice test.

Reading my son's multiple-choice study guide, I realized that most of the test-taking strategies and skills were a way of life for me, thought processes I had cultivated along the terrain of my children's developmental odyssey. I had developed the tools to identify a broad range of choices in any situation, and the mental flexibility to know there were probably yet more choices to consider. Having Plans B, C and D at the ready became second nature to me, and consequently, I rarely felt stuck or stumped in nasty or problematic situations.

This is the power of choice—the fusion point where recognizing the full diversity of opportunity joins forces with the ability to choose. These are the ultimate power tools. They are simple and timeless and perpetually abundant and free for the taking.

1. **Know the material**

   This means knowing your child and her specific needs and preferences so you can reject "everyone does it this way" options. It also means knowing and respecting your own risk tolerance, and the pace at which you best process cognitive and emotional information.

2. **Frame choices within The Big Picture**

   Everything we do, every choice we face, happens within the context of not just the moment, but the bigger picture. Applying the "Does it matter?" test can greatly reduce the load of choices you make, because a startling amount of the time, the honest answer to "does it matter?" is no.

3. **Identify the issue**

   Don't jump to apply solutions to a problem that may not

exist. For example, putting an autistic child on a restricted diet without concrete indication that it's needed may serve only to reduce the number of foods the child finds acceptable, without any particular benefit.

4. **Identify the broadest range of choices**

Realize that even when you feel you've exhausted the options, there are probably more choices. Enlist the help of others you trust to brainstorm with you. Wherever possible and appropriate, include your child in the discussion. The perspective of even very young children can be acutely on the mark.

5. **Apply common sense**

It's been said that common sense isn't common these days. Let's not forget that like so many critical thinking skills, common sense isn't something you're born with, but rather something you learn through the aggregation of experience, yours and other people's. It's the ability to understand and make sound decisions about practical matters large and small, through an alchemy of observation, perception, reflection, evaluation and cognition. It's available in unlimited quantity to anyone who chooses to hone it, and it will be one of those most potent tools in your decision-making cache.

6. **Reposition choices as true-or-false questions**

Reframing the choices as true or false may reveal your answer. Example: "XYZ therapy is always useful for autistic children" (or its cousin, "XYZ therapy is best for autistic children"). Reframed: "True or false: XYZ therapy would be beneficial for my child."

7. Beware of absolutes

"Always" and "never" are extremes that seldom apply. It only takes one exception to negate an always or a never. Think critically.

8. Use the process of elimination

Keep choices in context. Activities, treatments or therapies than impose excessive burdens on the family budget, schedule, space, or patience can't realistically be sustained. Evaluate as objectively as possible whether the expected benefit of such choices is realistic and/or worth it.

9. Make an educated guess

Sometimes you have to "take the test"—make a choice before you're done studying. Assemble the resources and information you do have and use what you've learned to that point (pro/con lists can be helpful), factoring in what you know to be your own abilities, strengths, and limitations. Consider which choices meet the bar for common sense.

10. Ignore distractors

This includes fear-mongering or scare tactics, small sample "studies" and "research," pressure to participate in "everyone does it" activities or events that are detrimental to you child, people who dismiss or sabotage your goals for your child, "must-have!" gadgets or treatments that sound like snake oil or hucksterism to you. To minimize distractions, establish parameters and focus on the task at hand. Prioritize goals, keep materials you need to meet those goals organized. Distance yourself from toxic people and situations.

11. "Look for the oddball."

I flinched at this when I first saw it, because I don't consider our kids to be oddballs. But giving it a broad definition yields the valuable perspective that the one, unusual solution that's overlooked or isn't feasible for most families just might be the one that works best for yours.

12. Pace yourself

Set incremental, achievable goals, prioritizing them to avoid overload and overlap. Learn when to listen more than talk, when and how to say no, when to slow down. Be realistic in setting time frames; build in buffers that assume everything will take longer than you think.

13. Trust your instinct

The first piece of parenting advice I ever received has been one of the most enduring. "There are a hundred ways to do any given thing parents have to do," our first pediatrician told me. "Only thirty of them will even make sense to you. Only ten will be anything you might consider trying, and you might try maybe three of those. If you're lucky, one of them will work. The most important thing is—trust your instinct. You know more than you think you know."

14. Do your best

Some years ago I was advised to not tell my children to "do their best," because "best" isn't measurable and therefore causes kids anxiety. To me, that was the tail wagging the dog. Doing your best, and teaching your child to do the same, means knowing yourself and building the self-confidence to stretch yourself in acceptable ways. It means knowing that doing your best isn't an absolute state of being, that it can, will, and should change by the hour, the situation, the year.

So there are your power tools. One of the best things about these skills? They're transferrable. Once you've learned them, you can instill them in your child. What more valuable legacy with which to endow her than the capacity for assessing every opportunity to reach the highest level of self-sufficiency she possible can, to enjoy the productive, meaningful adulthood to which every person is entitled.

And who knows but that during the long run-up to adulthood, your child might even use these life skills to pass a few of those confounded multiple-choice tests.

It continues ...

S hortly after graduating from high school, Bryce adopted a new mantra. "Everyone evolves" became his frequent commentary on the changes transpiring in his own life and the lives of those in the concentric circles rippling around and away from him. When your child is young and his challenges many, imagining him as an adult is a far stretch. But it comes all too soon. The simple messages of childhood collide with the oil-and-water social-emotional brew of adolescence. And the older your child grows, the more she must navigate on her own, and the more her ability to self-advocate becomes critical. Her success as an adult will depend upon her being able to describe the aspects of her autism that impact her ability to learn, communicate, and socialize, to be able to ask for the kind of help she needs, and be able to evaluate her choices in any situation and choose wisely.

Barring unthinkable catastrophe, your child with autism *will* become an adult. His responsibility for decision-making on his own behalf will skyrocket. In the eyes of the law (speaking of American law), it happens the moment the clock strikes midnight on the morning of his eighteenth birthday. Many services will fall away, many legal rights (and liabilities) will be his. Without your knowledge, permission, or approval, your child will be able to vote, marry, sign a contract, join the military. He'll be subject to adult laws and law enforcement, will be able to buy tobacco and pornography, consent to or decline medical treatment. You will no longer be able to even discuss his health with his doctor without his written permission. This isn't to say you won't continue to play a significant role in your child's life, advising, guiding, and supporting him. But your power to control the events of his life will diminish profoundly.

139

Preparing your child for a productive and self-sufficient adulthood begins the day he's born. Because the quality of his tomorrow depends on each today that comes before it, the question of the day, every day, is *how* will your child turn eighteen—prepared (or at least on the way), or naïve, unskilled, and ill-equipped to make the decisions that will fall to him?

The process of guiding your child with autism to adulthood is fraught with sly subtleties. It's influenced by not just the deliberate choices you make and actions you take, but also those you don't take, or take without careful consideration, the things you say or don't say, the perspectives you inhabit, the attitudes you project, knowingly or unintentionally. So before your child leaves childhood behind, there is one more thing this mother of an adult child with autism wants you to know.

Preparing your child for a productive and self-sufficient adulthood begins the day he's born.

Your child or student will become a reflection of your perspective and the perspective of those who teach and guide him, a person shaped by the choices you make and by how effectively he's taught to make sound decisions of his own. "Whether you think you can or whether you think you can't, you're probably right." For your child, as for yourself, Henry Ford's words come back to us again and again as a simple truth: that it is choice, not chance, that guides our hand on the helm.

Perspective is an amalgam of attitude, intention, empathy, and information—or the lack thereof. Whether deliberate or unconscious, the perspective you form about your child, his autism, his future, and the role you play in his life colors all you do and say, and creates the prism through which you present your child and yourself to the world.

"Your life is what your thoughts make of it," observed Marcus Aurelius. We must extend that: your child's life is what your thoughts make of it. More than any treatment, diet, or therapy, the perspectives from which we view a child's autism have the greatest impact on to what extent he'll learn to grow, thrive, and be a happy person. If we can't see our autistic child as an inherently capable, interesting, and valuable member of the family, the classroom and the community, no amount of education or therapy we layer on is going to matter.

> **If we can't see our child as inherently capable and interesting, no amount of education or therapy we layer on is going to matter.**

Our children depend upon us to create in ourselves and in others a perspective that empowers rather than obstructs. *We choose.* "Without feelings of respect, what is there to distinguish men from beasts?" asks Confucius. Any growth we hope to encourage in our children, and any consideration for them we hope to engender in others has to start from a position of respect and the choices and actions to fortify it.

In a sweet vignette I read many years ago, an American couple travelled to Capri where, in a tiny café perched on a towering cliff, they met a man who claimed to speak English. The couple understood not a syllable of the stream of words pouring out of the man as he led them to a balcony with a view of a steaming Mt. Vesuvius and the glittering Gulf of Naples. There, he gestured to the breathtaking grandeur and exclaimed, "Da panoram, she is so *very!*"

The diction and grammar may have been crude, but the man's perspective and intent were crystal clear. He wanted visitors to his beloved homeland to take in all the eye could see, because the more they looked, the more they'd see, the more they'd marvel, the more they'd find to do and the more they'd want to stay and do more. Your child's autism is like that. It invites you to live in the perspective of a flexible thinker and seeker, curious, engaged, and always wondering, envisioning, and doing all you can to expand life's experiences, for the child, for the family, and then by example, for others not involved with autism. Only by widening your own perspective can you inspire the child to do the same, that he may see himself as so much more than his autism, that he may embrace and live the conviction that the "panoram" life offers can be so *very*.

Bryce stood in the kitchen some months after graduation, chugging orange juice and loading slices of cheddar cheese onto sourdough bread. With the clarity that often comes with time and distance, he told me that he had spent his high school years trying to define himself. How would he fit into a world that viewed him as different, yet remain true to the vision of himself that he'd cultivated so carefully, and liked?

A fine line walked by many, I started to say. But I should have known that he had arrived there ahead of me. His smile, small but heart-melting, leaked quiet and comfortable self-confidence. He said:

"I knew I wasn't 'autistic' and I knew I wasn't 'normal,' whatever that is, so I chose something else. I chose to be optimistic. That's how I define myself."

Questions for Discussion and Self-Reflection

Chapter One

- In your experience, does hearing the term "autism" automatically bring up associations of limitations or "less than" among the general public, or among other parents, educators, or the media? Give several examples of preconceived notions you or others associate with the word "autism."

- The author suggests, "…what you choose to believe about a child's autism may be the single biggest factor affecting his ultimate outcome." Do you agree or disagree? Why?

Chapter Two

- Why does the author suggest throughout the book that sensory issues be the first consideration and accommodation made for the child with autism or Asperger's?

- Identify three settings or situations where sensory overload might cause your child or student to melt down or otherwise react negatively (flee, shut down).

- What accommodations can you make to home or school environments to ease your child's hyper- and/or hyposensitivities?

- Discuss the different ways your child's sensory sensitivities affect his or her learning abilities in a group setting.

Chapter Three

- In light of reading this chapter, describe specific instances in which your perception of your child or student's behavior has shifted from "won't" to "can't."

- In what ways might your own behavior toward your autistic child or student be confusing, illogical, negative, or unsupportive?

- How does a parent or teacher determine whether a child on the autism spectrum is being manipulative with behavior or is truly in need of assistance in understanding the situation at hand?

- What strategies have you developed to help yourself get through difficult moments so you can be a "can do" parent or teacher?

Chapter Four

- For the next few days, keep track of your own and your family's usage of imprecise language. Rephrase idioms, metaphors, slang, puns, etc. in concrete language. How does this awareness change the way you communicate with your child or student? How does it change his response to you?

- Discuss ways you can demonstrate, in verbal and nonverbal ways, that you are listening and hearing what the child is trying to communicate.

- Create a short list of communication strategies you could post in the classroom or at home to help others be more effective communicators with your child or student.

Chapter Five

- Discuss the different perceptions of ability people hold about children with autism who are nonspeaking versus those who have oral speech.

- Discuss the difference between talking and communicating.

- List five nonverbal communication behaviors that are frequently used during conversation. How many of these behaviors can your child or student demonstrate appropriately?

- Is teaching these nonverbal forms of communication included in the child's IEP? If not, why?

Chapter Six

- Identify three visual supports in your own life (calendar, cookbook, map, watch, etc.). How effectively could you function without them?

- What types of visual supports are used in your child or student's classroom? In the home? Other venues? What level of ongoing teaching is provided on how to use the visual support?

- Discuss how visual tools support and build a child's ability to perform tasks independently and interact socially.

- Do you feel the use of visual supports draws undesirable attention to the child with autism as having a disability? If so, what technology or other options might be used instead to ensure the same level of visual support?

Chapter Seven

- Draw a vertical line down the middle of a piece of paper. Write your child or student's name at the top. Title the left column "can do" and the right column "can't do." Set a timer for five minutes and list things the child can do on the left side. Set the timer again and complete the right column. Did your ideas stop before the timer went off? Entertain reasons why. Use this exercise to consider how easy/difficult it was to complete one side versus the other and what that may demonstrate about your perspective toward the child.

- How could you channel your child or student's strengths into opportunities for learning, recreation, or socialization?

- Can you identify your child or student's primary learning style?

- Discuss or reflect upon the more prevalent nay-sayer comments you've heard about what a child with autism will "never do." How many of these do you consider to be true about your own child or student?

Chapter Eight

- Discuss what it means to have "good social skills."

- Why is teaching social skills by rote practice not enough?

- To what extent do you assume children with autism or Asperger's will learn social skills by being around and watching other children? How does that assumption impact the way you teach social learning?

- Discuss the difference between teaching social skills and teaching for social competence.

- List the different social abilities needed to successfully function in a group setting. Discuss to what extent your child or student has these abilities and can use them in real-time social encounters.

- Identify several ways in which social skills differ

  ○ from culture to culture

  ○ from setting to setting (home, school, church, park, visiting others' homes)

  ○ from relationship to relationship (family member, classmate, teacher, stranger)

- When you teach a social skill, to what extent do you also teach why the skill is important to the child himself and to others, and how it makes others feel, react, and respond? If you do so infrequently, discuss possible reasons this may be so and how to turn that around.

Chapter Nine

- Have you tried to squelch a particular behavior in your child or student without identifying or addressing its source? What was the result?

- Describe a behavior of your own that you want to change. What need does it fill? Have you tried to extinguish the behavior? What did you try? How well did it work? Relate this to your efforts to change a behavior in your child or student.

- How might physical or physiological factors trigger your child or student's behavior? What steps could you take to determine this?

- How might emotional factors trigger your child or student's behavior? What steps could you take to determine this?

- What household or classroom rules do you enforce regarding respectful treatment of each other? Are there different standards for adults and children? Why?

- How important is it to model the behaviors you want from your child or student?

Chapter Ten

- What does "unconditional love" mean to you?

- Are you able to love your child or student unconditionally? Do you believe it's necessary or desirable? Why or why not?

- Do you or did you once view your child's autism as a tragedy? Has your thinking changed over time? How? Why or why not?

- How do you demonstrate acceptance of differences within your immediate family?

- The author suggests there is no "end of the road" when dealing with a child's autism. How does that idea make you feel?

The Sum of *Ten Things*: Your Power of Choice

- To what extent does the fear of making a wrong choice affect your decision-making?

- In what areas of your life do you consciously or unconsciously allow others (teachers, therapists, family members, etc.) to make choices about the health, education, and well-being of your autistic child? Identify one area that you would like to change, and brainstorm two things you could do to bring about this change.

- Describe a situation with your child when you felt you had no choices. After reading this chapter, can you describe other choices you may have had but didn't realize them at the time?

- Which of the fourteen strategies (power tools) the author offers for making choices resonate most strongly with you? Which seem hardest? Why?

Follow-up questions

- Prior to reading this book, what expectations did you have for your child or student with autism? Did anything in the book change your expectations? How? Did anything reinforce your existing thoughts?

- Prior to reading this book, what beliefs did you hold about autism in general? Did anything in the book change your beliefs about autism? How? Did anything reinforce your existing thoughts?

- If you were to hand this book to a friend or colleague, which points would you most want to convey?

- Will your child or student's life be different as a result of you reading this book? Will yours?

Acknowledgments

This marks the sixth time Veronica Zysk and I have collaborated on a book, and if the universe smiles on me, it won't be the last. Without her recognizing the fecundity of the ideas in my head and drawing them out, none of those books would have happened, none of the connections we've forged with families and professionals around the world would have resulted in the conversations we're having today. She continues to be my muse and soul sister. Several books ago, I ran out of superlatives for what her work and solidarity mean to me, to my work, and ultimately, to you, dear readers.

My thanks go to Jennifer Gilpin-Yacio and everyone at Future Horizons who make my books not only possible but successful. Thank you also to my agent Judy Klein, the force behind bringing dozens of translations of *Ten Things* to families around the world.

My husband Mark has always supported my work unconditionally, a gift beyond measure and one that no writer should ever take for granted.

Without my boys there would, of course, be no book. Connor and Bryce, you have always been the delightful, consummate embodiment of the words of one of my own favorite authors, Mark Twain: "My mother had a lot of trouble with me, but I think she rather enjoyed it!"

About the Author

An internationally renowned author, Ellen Notbohm's work has informed, inspired, and delighted millions in more than twenty languages. In addition to her four perennially popular award-winning books on autism and her multiple-award-winning novel *The River by Starlight*, her articles and posts on such diverse subjects as history, genealogy, baseball, writing and community affairs have appeared in major publications and captured audiences on every continent.

Web: ellennotbohm.com

Facebook: Ellen Notbohm, Author

Instagram: Ellen Notbohm

Twitter: @EllenNotbohm

LinkedIn: Ellen Notbohm

Pinterest: Ellen Notbohm